Praise for *Rogue L*

Paul draws on his significant experience as a senior leader in a highly successful international coaching consultancy as well as his more personal journey as a comic to share intriguing and practical ways in which leaders can initiate and lead change—and get great results. His humanity and desire to help shine through in this must-read from the front line of change leadership.

—**David Webster, Managing Director, Centre for Teams, London**

When we have reached the point in our growth and maturity, where we actively make use of adversity, or as the book subtitle states, "headwinds," to drive our own growth and the organization's innovation and creativity, we have risen above the blame-game and fear-driven reactions, and become high-performing, resilient, agile, motivated, and purpose-driven leaders. *Rogue Leadership* provides an excellent roadmap to your leadership growth journey with relevant examples and action-focused tools.

—**Sandja Brügmann, Managing Partner, the Passion Institute**

One of the things I like most about the advice in *Rogue Leadership* is that it's universal . . . equally applicable to the management of any sized organization, in any industry, and from anywhere in the world. That's because it's drawn from firsthand practice in dozens of organizations across the globe, private and public. There's nothing "theoretical" contained in these pages. It's all hard-won experience, translated into practical advice.

—**Tony Shaw, Founder and CEO, Dataversity**

Rogue Leadership maps out a clear-cut process to ensure performance and a transformed workplace. Insightful, funny and authentic reflection backed by thirty successful years across industries and boundaries.

—**Ethan Zohn, global philanthropist, leadership coach, two-time cancer survivor, and winner of "Survivor: Africa"**

As a female thought leader and entrepreneur I always appreciate a style management that begins from the inside out. Paul's ability to take leadership from the conference room to the comic's stage is brilliant way of introducing a new management style set for the future.

—**Tracy Kemble, PhD, Owner, Dr. Tracy TV and Mrs. Globe**

Rogue Leadership really dives into the depths of leadership and how it is comprised and created.

—**Steele Platt, Founder, Yard House**

I spent more than twenty years in the Marine Corps, but that didn't prepare me for leadership in a corporate world. Paul was my first boss. What a great ride! I had the benefit of learning directly what Paul has crammed into these pages. So many concepts, but the clarity of instruction gives any leader plenty to think about. It all starts with knowing themselves, the internal voice that they listen to. As Paul succinctly states, it's not about thoughts, but actions and consequences. Sharpen your mind as you browse Paul's buffet of leadership wisdom, earned the hard way through thirty years of practice. The rogue leader is the one who shapes the future. Is that you?

—**Craig Martelle, international best-selling author**

Rogue Leadership is very well written, easy to read and entertaining. A very important book on leveraging performance. A subject many companies and leaders themselves struggling with, given the complexity of business today.

—**Annelie Gullström, global digital and
business transformation expert**

Maybe experts don't always have the right answers. Some of us are meant to take the road less traveled and pursue opportunity others dismiss as too outlandish, too risky. Rosenberg articulates a convincing argument for listening to your gut. This book will help you find out if rogue leadership is in your DNA and how to flex your leadership muscle to challenge the status quo.

—**Frank Pietrucha, President, Definitive Communications,
and author, *Supercommunicator: Explaining the
Complicated So Anyone Can Understand***

In this book Paul empowers you to trust in your intuition to fulfill your leadership potential. With a strong emphasis on cultivating our authenticity, Paul demonstrates the power we've had all along, resides internally, within the seams of our idiosyncrasies. We just have to invest in our autonomy to activate it. In being rogue, we're being revolutionary!

—**Caroline McMenamin, Founder, Replenish:
Acting on Mental Health**

You can't have a more salient and current focus than *Rogue Leadership* does, given the times we live in. The maelstrom of the modern world—constant online communication, demands of the market, shareholders, and directors—creates pressure for everyone in an organization to perform at a pace on the edge of intolerable. *Rogue Leadership* offers a lucid path forward to confront the challenges leaders face, together with their employees, to reach their objectives without forfeiting sustainability. All while engaging the team around them and generating a work culture and climate that supports executing objectives and realizing high performance together.

—**Alejandra Sabugo, Gerente de Administracion, CMPC Tissue**

ROGUE
LEADERSHIP

Harnessing Headwinds to
Drive Performance

PAUL ROSENBERG

Published in the US by
Tertia Oculus Business Synergies™
Address: 4581 Weston Rd. Suite #320 Weston FL 33331 USA
Email: paulrosenberg.leadership.biz@gmail.com
Website: www.rosenbergpaul.com

First published in the US 2019
Copyright © 2019 by Paul Rosenberg

Rosenberg, Paul
Rogue Leadership, Harnessing Headwinds to Drive Performance

ISBN: 978-0-692-18546-9

Cover layout and design by Victoria Cooper at thebookcoverdesigner.com
Book typesetting by Nelly Murariu at pixbeedesign.com

Printed in the United States of America

Disclaimer
The names of some of the individuals have been changed to protect their privacy.

For Mauge, Pilar, and Fabi
Mis tres chicas lindas and the loves of my life

CONTENTS

CONTENTS

CONTENTS

ACKNOWLEDGMENTS

Nothing is ever done in a vacuum, and this book is no exception.

I'd first like to thank my colleagues, team members, employees, and clients for teaching me how important it is to listen, take risks, and do things differently, in spite of fears and concerns. The business world continues to be a great classroom, and I'm fortunate to have had many inspiring teachers throughout the years.

What I have learned in living on almost every continent and working in multiple industries is that the humanity in all of us is the foundation for change and performance, and we each have our unique ways of getting there. If we can do so with heart and have some fun along the way, even better.

A lot of people leaned in and helped me with their ideas, feedback, and quotes. Too many to name here, but you know who you. I am so grateful for your input and support.

I had some great role models and teachers growing up. Kati Pressman, my mom, was an author, improv actress, nurse, and all-around rabble rouser. My sister, Hyla, taught me the power of reflection and slowing down. My brother, David, has been a writer since the age of five and an inspiration to me. Howard Rosenberg, my dad, led by taking action for those who had no voice.

A special shout out to international best-selling author Craig Martelle, who urged me to put pen to paper. To my author friends, thank you for showing me the way. To Jimmy Calano, I appreciate your honesty and frank feedback.

ACKNOWLEDGMENTS

The global leaders who responded to my personal request for their wisdom and insights: Your contributions have added so much value to this project. You have inspired me.

Special thanks to my editors who worked tirelessly to help me tell a stronger story, communicate with more clarity, and make the message accessible to more than the voices in my head: twin brother screenwriter/author David Rosenberg for the rough draft and Christian de Quincey for the nitty gritty sentence-by-sentence work.

A big round of applause for editor and publishing consultant Sandra Jonas, who took the book to the finish line. Without your candid and insightful work, this book would still be ideas waiting on my laptop. Thank you for your patience and insistence that the hard work be done.

Finally, my thanks to every reader who has picked up this book. I hope that it contributes to your journey in a meaningful and enjoyable way.

PREFACE

On a rainy night in New York in the late '80s, Pablo, an up-and-coming young manager in the training and conference business, hopped into a cab and shared his ride to the airport with a stranger, who turned out to be an established global businessman. They immediately found common ground in the world of international commerce.

During their chitchat on the long ride to JFK, the businessman said he had a tip about the next great global opportunity: the Soviet Union. Certain that the markets would open up for the long term under Gorbachev, he seemed confident that astute entrepreneurs would make a killing in this untapped market.

The young manager got on his flight to Madrid and settled into his travel routine. Later, he thought about what his cab companion had said. *That guy might be right*, he said to himself, then leaned against the window and dozed off.

When he landed, he called his boss and recounted what the man had said. "What do you think"?

"Hate to disappoint you, Pablo, but that's an impossible pipe dream. It would take a ton of money and effort. It will never happen."

Over the next few days, Pablo sought additional feedback from colleagues, and they all expressed the same discouraging view:

"It's too far away and a different culture."

"It has never been done before, and it would take a long time just to get the door open."

"The Soviets control the ruble, an unstable currency."

"You don't speak Russian."

"Why take the risk?"

Pablo decided to seek advice from a friend outside his company. She simply asked him, "What does your gut tell you?"

"I don't have a clear grasp of the opportunity," he said. "But I want to pull the thread and see where this goes."

"That's your answer."

Over the next weeks, Pablo mustered the courage to pay a visit to the USSR embassy in Madrid and meet the consul for economic development. The introductory meeting went well. Pablo talked about doing a joint venture on business and marketing training and seminars. The consul expressed interest in the proposal, and they both agreed to be in touch. Nothing more happened for two months.

One day, Pablo just *knew* he had to return to the embassy and talk to the consul. His inner voice was quite strong and clear. "Wait here for an hour," the consul told Pablo when he arrived. "I have press interviews with the chief economic advisor for Gorbachev, one of the architects of *perestroika*."

The consul finally appeared and led Pablo into the garden, where the advisor waited. The three had a private one-hour meeting and discussed training, in particular the emerging need in the USSR for skills in two key areas: marketing and leadership.

They engaged in robust dialogue: "How can leaders move their organizations to a better place? What keys do leaders use to ensure marketing success? What tangible tools exist for business development?"

Fast-forward a year, and Pablo was in Moscow. He had listened to his gut and negotiated one of the first joint ventures on marketing training in the former USSR. Over several months, while negotiating the joint venture, he had led a number of workshops on leadership and marketing. Although Pablo's bosses eventually withdrew from the venture due to a lack of capital, that one taxicab conversation had yielded tangible results.

In the story above, Pablo is me.

I learned a lot from those events, as well as from many other business projects over the years and across the globe. Those experiences form the basis of this book. By going against the grain, by listening to my instincts and not following all the experts, and, most importantly, by taking meaningful action, I seized golden opportunities that others merely talked about or completely ignored.

I also failed—a lot. Each time I failed, I welcomed the lessons and adjusted my course. Over time, I developed a new definition for effective leadership—and acquired valuable tools to last a lifetime.

INTRODUCTION

Lead Powerfully by Going Rogue

Despite my many years of coaching, leading transformation, and change management, I am always amazed by how much energy, time, and money are invested in unlocking the enigma of powerful leadership: "What can we add to give us the advantage?" "Where is the next accelerator?" "How can we leap ahead of our competitors?"

The pace of new technology magnifies this dilemma. The demands of a high-tech world drive us to make faster decisions—we need to process information in a fraction of a second and be agile in how we lead our teams.

The multitasking options that face most leaders today boggle the mind. Constantly distracted by messages on mobile devices, they have to remain decisive, motivate their teams, align and balance competing demands—all while meeting the challenges of innovation.

In other words: *leaders need to be superheroes* (cape optional).

Many of us tend to look for something "out there"—some Holy Grail—to hang on to as a rock or support. While I firmly believe in getting outside help, the last thirty-plus years have taught me an important lesson: Looking only *outward* for solutions doesn't work. I have found that most of what we need lives right inside us. I call it *rogue leadership*.

This type of leadership involves acting—proacting not reacting—in strategic, meaningful, and purposeful ways. It also often involves taking the road less traveled and challenging the status quo.

TAKING CONTROL BY LETTING GO

"Decisive" leaders take action. But "effective" leaders, those who inspire their teams, focus on taking the *right* action, not just responding. Unfortunately, many of today's leaders act too quickly, showing little regard for how their actions will play out. Successful leaders, on the other hand, evaluate how their decisions will affect the system as a whole—and then they act.

We need effective, not decisive leadership.

I realize this might seem counterintuitive, but letting go of the need to respond, even for a moment, gives us more time for clarity and focus, as well as for reflection.

This book outlines how to develop a new leadership mindset and demonstrates the connection between that mindset and performance. First and foremost, this path begins by "going within" to find and use the tools we all have inside: the innate wisdom, accessed through intuition, that no external process or model can provide. The path also involves throwing away old paradigms and assumptions to create more powerful results.

I want to be clear: I do not reject or deny that external solutions can have value. But if the solution doesn't arise from within, true and deep change will not occur. What you as a leader personally bring to your team and organization—as well as what they bring to you—makes the difference.

"Insight" means "internal vision." Some of the best leaders in history had well-developed gut instincts. Take, for example, John F. Kennedy and his handling of the Cuban Missile Crisis. Leaders like JFK take risks, innovate in spite of resistance and ridicule, and see beyond what others consider "normal." We use phrases such as "she sees the big picture" or "he is a visionary," which imply that people have the ability to see beyond what lies in front of them. You need such insight to succeed as a leader.

Leadership at Sony Corporation provides another good example. In the '60s, the slogan "Made in Japan" indicated poor quality and cheap goods. Sony's leaders had vision, and they decided to change that reputation by building a business empire based on high standards. Collectively and individually, they saw something beyond the obvious and immediate.

"Okay," I hear you say, "I get vision, but what about instinct and gut?"

A friend of mine knew Steve Jobs during Apple's formative years and was invited to join the fledgling company. He thought about it for a few days and then said no. Relying on logic, not his gut, he used facts and risk management to make his decision. He jokingly tells me that every day he wakes up, splashes water on his face, looks in the mirror, and says, "You are a f#@*ing idiot!" He didn't trust his gut, which told him to accept.

Another example: When the internet first rolled out, no one saw its use beyond initial defense or security applications except for a few early adopters and innovators. The people who "got it" encountered a lot of initial resistance. Similar breakthroughs happened in voice-recording technology, originally designed for dictation. In every case, someone had to see beyond what everyone else saw.

Effective leaders also understand the value of *balance*. We know from biology that if too much energy accumulates in one area of the body, it creates an equally destructive imbalance or counter-reaction. When leaders throw more hours and attention at one problem, they naturally focus less on other issues. Working long hours and weekends is fine in short bursts, but a long-term lack of attention on other parts of the business will cause greater problems.

With hundreds of emails a day, multiple meetings, the clamor for big data and instant decision-making, something has to give—usually *effectiveness*, along with the ability to recognize opportunities and capture them.

So how do we achieve balance? Of course, as leaders, we want it all nicely packaged—for example: "Ten Keys That Will Unlock Success," "The Seven Habits of Highly Effective People." "Ten Top Tips" . . . "Three French Hens" . . . "Fifty Ways to Leave Your Lover."

We want the fastest, easiest answer.

None exists.

Instead of a quick fix, we can all make use of our natural "leadership muscles" by strengthening and developing them over time. The pages that follow will show you how.

CORE ROGUE LEADERSHIP TRAITS

This book will show you how to think and act like a rogue leader. Rogue leaders tap into their intuition, welcome new ways of operating, look for ways to optimize tools and processes, and manage change with a distinctive style.

They also show up with purpose, communicate simply, lead from the heart, and work tirelessly to empower their workforce.

This is not a one-size-fits-all book of solutions. You are unique, as are your organization's challenges. Though not all the insights offered here may apply to you, I trust you will find grains of wisdom that will serve you and challenge your current mindset. My goal is to start a conversation with you that I hope will move you to a better place, both in the workplace and beyond.

Together, we will explore tangible and successful approaches you can apply to leading your people and your business. While you might not embrace all the suggestions offered here, nevertheless they all remain essential to any leader's ability to transform. The book focuses on *transformative leadership*, not merely on leadership. It's about effectively changing the course of your team or organization—it's about changing *objectives* and improving *results*.

PART 1

EMBRACING YOUR INTUITION

You have to leave the city of your comfort and go into the wilderness of your intuition. What you'll discover will be wonderful. What you'll discover is yourself.

—**Alan Alda, actor**

FINDING THE "ONE THING"

Success demands singleness of purpose.

—Gary Keller, author

The outside world commands our attention and draws us in every day. Whether market pressures, staffing levels, endless meetings, or requests from the boss—almost anything can trigger the all-too familiar morning crisis.

Many leaders are moved and swayed by the fray. To effectively manage what happens in the professional world, we need to do the opposite by standing firm and acting from our foundation.

In the movie *City Slickers,* Mitch (Billy Crystal) makes a similar discovery, as lone-wolf cowboy Curly (Jack Palance) enlightens him:

Curly: "Do you know what the secret of life is?" He pauses a moment, then holds up one finger and states: "This."

Mitch: "Your finger?"

Curly: One thing. Just one thing. You stick to that and the rest don't mean sh*t.

Mitch: "But what is the 'one thing'?"

Curly: That's what you have to find out.

Curly's statement, both humorous and true, strikes a chord. Each of us has a different compass, and we lead people with different compasses. Successful leaders know how to align their teams' North Stars with their own, and they do that by first understanding themselves. If we just pay attention to the daily noise and don't have a guiding path and focus, we will not reach our destination.

If every action and decision we take is based on that core guiding principle, we ensure that we have alignment in all that we do. I liken it to a downhill ski run. The skier can take many different actions on the course, but the finish line remains the same. How you get to the finish line is up to you. Decide the principal guiderails first.

Two examples of the "one thing":

I had a long candid talk with one of my clients, a senior executive with a global leader. In his late forties, he had a great salary and perks. His guiding principle was time with his family, but he had reached a point in his career where the withdrawals (time away from his family) were more than the deposits (perks/shares/financial security). So, he left and gave up much of the golden parachute he was due if he had stuck around a few more years.

Another: One of my bosses mentioned that his work was all about creating memories for his clients and his team. That's what drove him. That was his one thing. As such, he focused on building robust connections, true partnerships, strong results, and shared stories that remain his legacy to this day.

Once we define our one thing, our intuition will let us know if we are straying away from it. When things don't feel right, when there is extra pressure, or events seem unsettling, we need to listen voices and impulses. It might be time to lean in by spending some time with ourselves.

ALONE AGAIN NATURALLY

The Power of Solitude

Without reflection, we go blindly on our way, creating more unintended consequences, and failing to achieve anything useful.

—Margaret J. Wheatley, author

By three methods we may learn wisdom: first, by reflection, which is noblest; second, by imitation, which is easiest; and third by experience, which is the bitterest.

—Confucius, philosopher

Today's world often feels like a feeding frenzy at an all-you-can-eat buffet. We will be full, but what did we eat? As inputs barrage us at an accelerated pace, our expectations for handling them increase accordingly.

How can we stop the daily grind of reacting and step away to *respond* in a more purposeful way that allows us to take back control?

Sandja Brügmann, a visionary leader of the Passion Institute, lays out the challenge clearly: "Once we have developed under-standing of how we interfere with our visions and goals, then comes the challenging process of unlearning and changing specific behaviors."

Unlearning takes hard work. "It requires one to move out of automatic behaviors and into conscious understanding, where we take control of our own actions and lives," notes Brügmann. "It requires confronting uncomfortable feelings and adopting an attentive vision for a different business life." In fact, it takes many of the same skills that entrepreneurs need to succeed in their businesses. "It's a real act of self-love at a deep level," she says. "It's also what you need to do to become a more effective leader."

According to Brügmann, to unlearn and become effective leaders, we must adopt behaviors that support solitude and reflection.

SOLITUDE

In *The Voice of the Dolphins and Other Stories* (Stanford University Press, 1992), Leo Szilard talks about removing yourself from your surroundings to find out who you have become. I can't think of a more powerful tool for a leader. By placing yourself in a different environment, you remove the background noise that may be influencing you.

When we look at the same things every day, we tend to stop *seeing* them. If you insert something new into the picture, you will notice more detail and understand your situation with more clarity.

Getting away for long periods can be difficult for most people, but even the busiest leaders find time to do so, especially when they face some tough decisions. They slow down, go for a walk, change locations, or turn off their phones.

Control the environment—don't let it control you. You aren't responsible for what is out there—but you are responsible for how you deal with it, process it, or act on it.

REFLECTION

A different environment allows you the space to reflect. Originating in Sweden with the consulting firm Leadership in Motion, action reflection learning (ARL) offers a methodology for thoughtfully reflecting on experience as an essential part of the learning process. At its core, it's taking the time to reflect before acting. Done well, this practice can help you derive greater meaning and understanding from a given situation.

In *Gentle Interventions for Team Coaching: Little Things That Make a Big Difference* (CreateSpace, 2013), author Ernie Turner focuses on the power of reflection:

> To reflect on something that happened helps us connect effects with causes, extract meaning, and learn from it. We can also learn about ourselves when we reflect on the responses we generate in others.

We have evolved with brains hardwired to react rather than going "within" and stopping that impulse. You will do well to practice reflection, giving yourself time to weigh pros and cons and make informed decisions.

Many of my colleagues use headphones to silence the noise around them, especially on planes. Why wouldn't you do the same for your business life? Shut out the world and take time to think and feel more clearly, paying attention to your own inner process. Again, slowing down in critical situations enhances your ability to take in the big picture.

When my new boss at RLG International told me I was being assigned to a new project in Chile, I soon found myself on a plane headed for Santiago. Like the plane I took to Madrid, it gave me an opportunity to listen to my instincts.

As I headed out that night, I felt deep regret. What had I done? What if I failed? What if I couldn't function in this new role as a coach? What about the new team? How would they feel about an American coming in? Noticing the chatter, I forced myself to quiet down.

Sure enough, I heard a calm and sure voice from within: "This should be interesting."

I'd felt trapped in a dead-end job, and the change forced me to develop new skills much more quickly than if I had brought along my own experience. The changed circumstances allowed me to remain present and to listen without any other voices—all because I had no preconceived ideas about what to do. I had the luxury of creating responses based on actual feedback from my environment.

As it turned out, the stint in Chile launched my role as an international leadership and performance coach. I also met my wife and daughter there. Pretty good decision!

One of the strongest and most successful innovators in the financial world I have ever met approaches everything with a measure of healthy skepticism. Although he trusts his gut absolutely, he approaches big, complex issues by giving himself time to sit with the project to let it take shape within him.

Few leaders can accomplish this under pressure. They jump into projects without sufficient preparation. If you are one of those rare individuals who can do well on the fly, good for you.

INNER VOICE

The Third Eye and Leadership

Don't let the noise of others' opinions drown out your own inner voice.

—Steve Jobs, entrepreneur

By creating space for solitude and reflection, you also clear the way to hear your inner voice. That can't happen unless you have some form of "noise cancellation." You have to consciously put that into place.

The third eye serves as a great symbol for inner wisdom. Whether or not you believe you have a third eye, it symbolizes our ability as humans to move beyond the norm.

What feels right? What choice could I make to feel better? Sit with these questions and see what shows up. Clear your mind, and perhaps listen to some music to shut out the intensity of your surroundings, pausing all the things you have to do.

Just because you can't hear your inner voice, or you ignore it, doesn't mean it isn't there.

A personal story might help here: My twin brother and I are basically on the same wavelength, so we experience telepathic connections and shared moments of experience.

Years ago, when I found myself caught in the middle of a police shootout with a sniper, I had unknowingly triggered a response a thousand miles away. As I witnessed two policemen get shot in front of me and then got trapped between the shooter and the SWAT team, my brother's pulse began to race and he felt death was imminent—as if he were there with me.

I know that all of us have the ability to tap into our gut and instinct, but too much noise prevents us from doing so effectively. I also know that we have the ability to connect telepathically at a distance, but many of us have never exercised it.

In modern industrial society, we tend to discount anything that is not "scientific" or logical—we want "proof." Yet day after day, many of us experience moments we call "miracles" or "paranormal" because we don't understand them (and many people fear what they don't understand).

Mainstream society ridicules interest in New Age practices that involve crystals, shamans, or Earth priestesses. I, too, have had to stifle the urge to joke here about such things. Yet with a sober and more open-minded perspective, I realize that people have used these practices for millennia—so I tend to think they likely contain some knowledge and wisdom.

It might not be wise to say "My gut tells me . . ." in front of your shareholders—even though I suspect many successful decisions have been based on gut instinct. I'm sure we have all seen examples of this in our professional lives. But we don't acknowledge it when it happens.

Based on conversations with people who use their inner voice a lot, I know that intuition and instinct do not always deliver precise information. Sometimes it's a vague feeling or a premonition, and other times the message comes through loud and clear: "take this path." A few of my colleagues make good use of intuition as one of many factors when making a decision. As a "tool," intuition or instinct can adapt to different circumstances.

So how do you actually connect to that resource—your innate intuition?

Some of my clients use notes or journals. Others go into solitude, as discussed in chapter 2. Still others shut the door to the office and reflect. Whatever works for you, be purposeful about it.

You don't need to contort your body into different yoga positions or engage in mental gyrations to access the "muscle" of intuition. You strengthen it by paying attention to how and what you feel and eventually to what your inner voice communicates.

Recreating a pathway takes time; repetition makes the difference. Combine reflection and solitude, and then listen for what emerges as you open up to your inner voice. The more you practice, the clearer your channel.

Have you ever tossed and turned over something? Does your mind keep going there? These could be signs that you need to listen more and pay attention to the feeling that doesn't go away.

Two of my favorite quotes on this:

> A voice in my head tells me that I'm at the twilight of an extraordinary life. I say extraordinary because of the people who have loved me. I say twilight because of what people say to me in the supermarket.
>
> **—Charles Nelson Reilly, actor**

> That inner voice has both gentleness and clarity. So, to get to authenticity, you really keep going down to the bone, to the honesty, and the inevitability of something.
>
> **—Meredith Monk, author**

DECISION-MAKING

Don't Box Yourself in a Corner

Quick decisions are unsafe decisions.

—**Sophocles, ancient Greek playwright**

When a decision must be made, rogue leaders know how to stop the impulse to respond right away. Even if someone says "I need an answer *now*," rogue leaders take their time to determine if the person really does need an immediate answer.

Push back on anyone who boxes you in a corner where you can't make an effective decision. More often than not, the people who make such demands think they need a decision right away, which is *their* pressure they want to transfer to you. Yes, our bosses, teams, and the public appreciate decisiveness, but when the stakes are high and everyone is demanding an immediate response, they aren't demanding the right solution. Instead, they are saying, "Do something now." And it will make them feel better.

If your inner voice tells you that doing something is better than doing nothing, tell it, "Time for a time out."

Listen to yourself first. Write down whatever emerges as possible courses of action—a good way to learn how to "hear" your gut and trust it.

If you really can't get that quiet, find one person in your circle who can reflect or "mirror" back to you what they hear, especially if you don't have the luxury of working with a good coach. You can make this mirroring practice part of your reflection process and incorporate it as part of your weekly routine.

I cannot overemphasize the importance of being willing to hear candid feedback. Although it might not ultimately change your decisions, it creates opportunities for new ideas to emerge. For the best results, you must suspend all judgments. This is hard to do because we naturally want to evaluate or compartmentalize.

Once you do, go out and ask a group of key people—your leadership team and a select few at all levels of your organization—to get their perspectives. Don't make the common mistake of asking only members of your leadership team to weigh in first. They might not offer the breadth and depth you want.

You don't have to do what they say, but rather, their feedback might lead to possibilities you hadn't thought of.

Remember the scene in *Apollo 13* where Ed Harris announces that their space module will run out of fuel and the young scientist says, "Power is everything. Power down everything." That was the solution they needed. As a leader, you can turn to your team for help—you don't have to make all the decisions on your own all the time.

When good leaders face high stakes, they combine their own inner evaluations with candid feedback from selected others. This prepares them to bring the issue to a wider audience and to open up ongoing dialogue.

To make the most beneficial decisions, first throw away assumptions, monitor and manage reactions, and listen to your business instincts. Then slowly bring in a diverse group of voices to create the plan. Not everything has to be answered yesterday.

Going inward can give clarity, remove unwanted noise, and yield better decisions. Solitude or a change in environment allows the inner voice, instinct, and third eye to be more available as everyday tools.

RECAP
Part 1: Embracing Your Intuition

1. Move yourself to a different environment, especially when you need to make big decisions.
2. Schedule "off time" that allows you to reflect and process. Add it to your calendar, and let your team know your off time is off limits.

3. Slow down.

4. Learn to say no. Choose to cancel out the noise.

5. Suspend judgment on all ideas and paths.

6. Go renegade: If you have the impulse to act, do nothing and sit on it for a while.

7. Take a long walk.

8. Postpone conversations if you need the time. People can accept "I can't right now, but I will get back to you at [a definitive time]."

9. Practice noticing what your inner voice tells you—write it down

10. Consider these questions: How do I feel? What do I hear? Do I feel confused or uncomfortable with what I think? How do I react?

11. Dig in or stay with the process until the discomfort clears.

12. Be open to your intuition—just because you honor it does not make you crazy or metaphysically gaga. (Practice this in private if you worry about your reputation.)

PART 2

CREATING NEW BEHAVIORS

To change a habit, make a conscious decision, then act out the new behavior.

—Maxwell Maltz, scientist

OLD DOGS *CAN* LEARN NEW TRICKS

They always say time changes things, but you actually have to change them yourself.

—Andy Warhol, artist

We often hear that leaders get stuck in their ways. Our collective consciousness holds fast to the idea that people don't change.

According to the old paradigm, our brains stop growing and changing at a young age, and very little can be done to alter the structure and dynamics of our brains and nervous system later in life. Modern neuroscience tells a very different story. Recent research now confirms the revolutionary idea of "neuroplasticity"—that our brains remain flexible and malleable throughout our lives. In other words, we can and do generate new pathways in our brains. And changes in our brains result in new behavior.

Neuroplasticity is the capacity of the brain to change its function through both mental and physical events. Prior to the "neuroplasticity revolution" beginning in 2007, scientists widely believed that the human brain remained "fixed" after early childhood.

Recent neuroplasticity research shows, for example, that long-term meditation actually "rewires" the brain. In other words, we now know we can intentionally change how our brains function by choosing to engage in different mental and physical exercises. You can change the way you feel, think, and behave.

If leaders and those they lead can unlearn bad behaviors, habits, and responses, then the possibilities for positive change can radically alter their organizations. Because of neuroplasticity, we do not need to remain slaves to the past—we can creatively and intentionally bring about a new and more productive future.

Change involves a disruption of sorts. Something new or different reorganizes energy, stops the current flow, and replaces it with something else. For change to occur and get established, we need to *experience* the difference—and that often involves a change of stimulus.

If leaders can consciously change the stimulus they receive, they can dramatically change their organization.

To create change in our brains, something must change physically—and because our brains and minds are intimately connected, the stimulus for neural change gets activated by emotions. As our emotions shift, our minds interrupt the nerve impulses sparking between the brain's synapses. This shift could come from a significant emotional event like an accident, or from an unanticipated response, like a call from a long-lost friend.

Before attempting to transform an organization, leaders need to embody the desired change themselves and manage their own responses first.

Here is a story that shows we can all change.

The day was long and memorable for all the wrong reasons. In three separate meetings, my client, a corporate leader, had lost his patience and yelled out profanities at his team and workforce. He had been combative the entire week. I didn't know him well, but as I observed him, I began to worry about how to stop his tirades. They just created ill will and frustration.

Two weeks before, we had met for the first time as client and coach. I was hired to support his program and help him accelerate performance. I could tell he was uneasy, but it wasn't clear why. On the positive side, he was willing to jump in and use my coaching to improve his team's performance, be more successful, and reach company objectives. He came across as both excited and measured at the same time.

I asked him about his vision for his legacy—he had been a leader for many years in major defense construction. Without hesitation, he answered, "I want to be known and remembered as the man who championed the workforce and brought them together to work with leadership to achieve goals and create a better workplace."

One of a rare breed of managers, he spent most of his time on the shop floor with the workers instead of in his office high above the construction area. This made him well-known in his industry.

After I watched him lose patience and control in the three consecutive meetings, my gut told me somebody had to give him feedback. He couldn't afford another tomorrow like today.

I called him. "Jack, we need to talk. You said your door was always open. I'm coming up."

"No, you are not."

"Can you please give me five minutes in person?"

"Not going to happen."

I knew that I had to give him the feedback right then. My inner voice urged me on—despite his high level of frustration, anger, and unwillingness to engage. How could I get him to a safe place and diffuse the barrage of negative energy?

I thought quickly and gently asked him not to hang up. "Can you give me five minutes now on the phone?"

"Okay."

I paused and reflected on what I should say. I needed to go where he was and to honor him. "Jack, what legacy do you want when you leave the company?"

"I want to be known and remembered as the champion of the workforce and a leader who led from the trenches with them and met our goals as the best in the business."

Bingo.

Feeling a little nervous, but with a calm, clear voice, I asked, "After today's three meetings, what do you think your legacy will be?"

Silence. Then he took a deep breath and whispered an expletive.

I let it be and let him be with that moment.

After a few seconds that seemed like an hour, he said, "I'll call you back later." He hung up but never called me back. And that was fine. I knew he had heard me.

The next day, as I went into his office for our morning huddle, he reached out his hand and said, "Thank you for talking me down off the ledge." His famous smile and energy had returned, radiant as it should be.

He was even more committed to reaching his objectives. He knew he had to change the way he communicated with his team. He apologized to every team member, both in group settings and individually, throughout the following two days.

We both learned some powerful lessons in this crisis:

1. Seek to understand and go to where that person is.

2. Move beyond emotions, however intense or thick they might be.

3. Listen to your inner voice, or at least consider it before taking any action.

4. Show up differently. Trust depends on presence and action, not on words. Jack worked hard to change his internal filter and communication style.

5. Be humble and cultivate the ability to recognize your own errors.

Because I honored Jack's values, he could hear me and process my feedback, creating a lifelong baseline of trust and candid communication between us. His willingness to "learn new tricks" made the difference. I knew he had my back, and he knew I had his. The tirades stopped, and he went on to lead a very successful program with his workforce. He is now retired, and his legacy truly lives on, as he wished.

Reconstructing new responses means taking risks, trying out new things, testing, and observing. The only way to change something that isn't working is to stop it, by either interrupting it or taking different actions. Recognizing and admitting we have a weakness or risk to deal with is often the challenge.

To recap: As humans, we can relearn anything or create new behaviors. The circuit has to be broken in some way—through failure, a new lesson, different actions, a crisis—something that takes our focus away from the present, even for a moment.

THE ACTION ILLUSION

Value-Added Execution

Appearances are often deceiving.

—Aesop, ancient Greek storyteller

We all get fooled every day by the world revealed through our senses. In the business world, we get fooled by the biggest behavior con of all: *activity.*

In business, we often assume that any action at all trumps staying put with the status quo. But sometimes we need "plateaus of peace"—moments or periods of stability and rest to recharge before the next burst of energy and action. Many folks believe they always need to act (think Type A personalities!). You could say that some people feel addicted to taking action. True enough— all change and progress require *action* of some kind. But taking action alone rarely achieves the desired result.

We tend to overlook the critical importance of *timing.* Because the entire world around us quivers with action and activity (mostly unseen), we need to skillfully time our actions to fit the rhythms of the systems we find ourselves in. Rogue leaders have great, instinctive timing.

Here is an example: One of my client's team members gave a presentation to the VP of her entire organization—an early adopter and fan of continuous improvement, or CI. As with other leaders I have worked with, she held the vision that one day they wouldn't need any separate department or initiative because that would be how they normally did business. They would improve naturally and continuously. She constantly communicated that message.

I spoke with the team beforehand, and I reinforced that they had to be able to express to the VP the value of their work, money, and effort. I felt intuitively that they needed to be aware of their audience, and not declaring victory without results that backed that premise up. It would be activity without added value.

The senior leader in charge of presenting updates chose not to listen. He ran through the statistics and proudly reported that they had more than one hundred improvement events in the past five years.

When the VP asked him for details, in actual dollars, of the return on investing in the CI training and program, the manager could not answer. Even though he hadn't taken the time to evaluate what the CI program did for their profitability, everyone seemed comfortable with the "spend." In fact, they held it up as a badge of honor to her. In reality, the program might not have added any value at all, as it wasn't being measured properly. It was the moment she lost confidence in their efforts.

I call this a "staticmatic" event—meaning that's as deep as it goes. Everyone can "check the box" and feel good about the volume. Measuring activity instead of measuring *results* clouds the judgment of many managers. As noted earlier, instead of "any action," we need to time the "right action."

Not all "activity" qualifies as right or value-added action.

Do you allow your team to be busy instead of being productive? Can you create more impact without spending more time?

I hear the same complaint across all cultures and multiple international assignments: "I am so busy, and my people are so busy. I don't have the time to do X." But if you continue this kind of approach, you will lose money and, perhaps, frustrate your workforce.

When your middle manager shows you a full calendar of to-dos, it fits your comfort zone. Meetings, events, and more meetings can easily camouflage unfocused activities. As a leader, get in the habit of asking yourself and your team, "What do we get out of spending all this time fulfilling our schedules?"

EMBRACING FAILURE AND RISK

I have not failed. I've just found 10,000 ways that won't work.

—Thomas A. Edison, inventor

I make mistakes like the next man. In fact, being—forgive me—rather cleverer than most men, my mistakes tend to be correspondingly huger.

—J. K. Rowling, author

The glass-framed board outside the CEO's office featured a nice framed photo of one of the employees. Beneath, engraved in big, bright letters, it proclaimed: "Failure of the Month." How do you react when you read this?

For most of us, the reaction would probably be laughter, a smile, or just plain incredulousness at the absurdity of such a thing.

Fear of failure drives so many of our actions. At a very young age, we begin to notice we get praise for doing well and feel shame when we miss the mark. Competition is good, but like sex, drugs, and alcohol (not rock 'n' roll), it's better in moderation.

The professional world puts a premium on success, driving us to shine and stand out. At the same time, we all need the space to fail and the ability to learn from our mistakes. We are so focused on the "wins," we don't give failure its proper due. As a result, we miss a lot of learning opportunities.

In other words, most leaders fail when it comes to failing.

Although it might sound like a paradox, failure should be celebrated in our success-obsessed culture. If handled right, mistakes and failure can guide us back on course.

Unless leaders develop and follow a purposeful approach to failure, using it as a catalyst or tool for improvement, their organization will continue to fail. Because that kind of environment is so common, very few people in business are willing to take risks, push the envelope, or try new ideas. To survive and thrive using this model, we must let go of all we know and approach challenges in a radically different way.

Our childhoods are defined by experimenting—trying, observing, and changing. But when we enter adulthood and become leaders, we move away from that, losing one of the most important traits that can bring about success.

When I was a kid and played around with my chemistry set, I blew up more than a few things—all in an exploratory spirit. In short, I didn't avoid mistakes and failure, but instead, I learned from them.

When one of the most brilliant business leaders I know sold his business for hundreds of millions of dollars, he succeeded because he paid attention to his failures. Risk-averse leaders block creativity and often get in the way of moving their business forward. Hockey player Wayne Gretsky's famous quote sums it up well: "I scored more goals because I took more shots."

We need to evaluate risk in a new light. If we truly want a different world, we have to tear down the old one. That can seem overwhelming to some people. But it doesn't have to happen overnight. It just has to happen.

Even if your current culture doesn't embrace risk and failure in a transparent way, you can still learn from the innovation that comes from a "think tank" environment. An effective solution would be to set up a standalone area or department as an incubator for new ideas where failure is allowed, and learning follows from trial and error.

But you don't need a formal incubator to learn from failure. Every organization can take steps every day to ensure they don't stifle innovation and performance. They achieve this by capturing and learning meaningful lessons.

Failure has been the greatest teacher in my life. My success rides on the fact that I have failed so many times. Often, I have either not known what I was doing or made colossal mistakes. I have been stupid, arrogant, overconfident, and hardheaded. Just to be clear, though: I am not asking for forgiveness.

I have picked out my top four failures. Grab some popcorn and enjoy my pain (my therapist says this will be good for me).

1. My Inner Idiot

I was new on the job in a fish-food plant that made pellets for salmon farms in Southern Chile. I saw the plant manager put a fish pellet in his mouth, bite it into two pieces to look inside. I didn't know what he was looking for, but he exuded confidence and knowledge (not to mention fish-meal breath!). In an attempt to get accepted by the new client, I followed suit. In front of the crew I was coaching, I reached into a barrel, pulled out a pellet, and bit down. The entire crew burst into laughter.

"Gringo, what are barrels for?"

I hadn't paid attention to the safety initiation, but then I remembered: "Um, rejected material?"

"That would be a yes, *compadre.*"

"Why was it rejected?" I asked nervously.

"Staph infection."

Then I burst out laughing, mortified and humbled, but enjoying the absurdity of the moment.

My response to my unhappy meal, as well as the crew's reaction, has served me well over the years. Here are the insights I learned:

- ✏ Laughing at your mistakes makes you human, and creates trust. If you handle the incident with grace, it adds to the folklore of shared experience at work. We not only remember great leaders and their performance, but also their goofball moments: "Remember when Ed accidentally

33

showed his vacation photo in his Batman speedo swim trunks?" It's always good to be part of the company legends—in a fun way.

✏ Being dumb also allows you to listen better, without your inner über-leader trying to prove how much you know by getting ready with your response. Communicating is not tennis. Unless your name is Serena.

✏ Asking "stupid" questions actually opens the way for creative thinking and can highlight issues everyone else might have dismissed—for example, asking, "Why are we doing this? Do we need to be on this path?"

✏ Being "dumb" and not knowing it all comes across as nonthreatening, and I have used it to build relationships. It helps us avoid triggering defense mechanisms in others.

According to some of my best mentors, "How you show up is how you show up." You can decide what that means for you. If you don't know how to fall on your sword when appropriate, leading may be difficult. Recognizing your errors and having accountability keeps you authentic. A colleague of mine once made a significant accounting error, but because she didn't try to hide it, it served her well in the eyes of the company. Doing this well can be an art form.

In case you were wondering, I never did get an infection.

2. Eating My Own Left Foot

One of my most endearing jobs involved working for an assistant to the mayor of a small city in California. I wrote speeches, served as his *aide de camp*, met with the public, and handled protocol at events. An exciting and interesting job—except for the weekly council meetings.

The mayor, one of the first Asian Americans in US politics, stood firm as a powerful voice against discrimination. Together, we made a great team, and we would often sit at his koi pond, feed the fish, and map out strategy.

For the Cinco de Mayo parade, I would usually ride with the mayor, but because of the vice mayor's Latino heritage, he was given that honor. The mayor bowed out and asked for a full report when it was over.

When the parade stopped in front of the grandstand, on impulse, the vice mayor and I decided to have a little fun and run around the car and change seats, much to the delight of the celebrating crowd.

After the parade, I went into the mayor's office and he asked how it went. With pride and excitement, I blurted out, "It was great, so funny! We decided to switch places, like a Chinese fire drill!"

The mayor remained silent for at least thirty seconds. "What about what you did makes it Chinese?"

He let me sit there for a few moments. I didn't have an answer. I realized I had offended him and an entire group of people. Language is important. He knew I meant no harm, but he also knew I would learn a great lesson that day about how to communicate. He raised my awareness with grace and wisdom, and for that I have been grateful ever since.

3. Crash and Burn: Cutting Losses

I sensed from the beginning that it would be a tough assignment. I had been brought in by a corporate leader, Bob, to help improve a maintenance turnaround schedule on a ship that needed to be back sailing as soon as possible. When I met his team leader, Alex, the head of operations, he said all the right things, but I could detect the insincerity in his voice. Although he had signed the contract, I was convinced that Alex did so only to please his boss.

At least I have the support of the top guy, I told myself. At the end of the first week, Bob invited me to dinner and told me he was leaving the company. Right away, my gut told me to withdraw, but I had just moved to a new country with my wife, gone independent, and invested a lot in this project.

I anticipated the conversation I would have on Monday with Alex. True to form, he told me Sunday night to be in his office first thing the next morning.

Alex sat me down and said he didn't want me there, that I would not succeed with the project, and now that Bob was gone, he was in charge. He asked for minimum interference with him and his team.

Instead of trusting my instincts, I stuck it out. Predictably, after six months, the project collapsed, in spite of some good work. I had tried ignoring his complaints for a few months, pushing harder, but it became impossible to continue. It took me a long time to realize that I couldn't be successful, because I wasn't given the space and support to do so.

4. The Five-Year Itch

My team's multi-year coaching engagement with a major client was coming to an end. While I made it clear that we eventually would have to leave the site, we had been a good partner for many years, and had done great work. The client acknowledged that his decision to move in another direction was not a reflection on me or the team I managed; he just wanted to take the project in-house. Fair enough.

We began the transition to develop that in-house capability—which would eventually eliminate the need for our consulting coaching services. Word came down from my bosses that they wanted one last proposal to do some other work there. My gut told me no, that we had been through enough, that things were going well with the exit, and that we were delivering what the client wanted.

I felt immense pressure to respond to their request anyway. What could it hurt? Instead of listening to my gut, I made the proposal, and all hell broke loose from the client team. They were offended that I was trying to sell them more business. It created an avoidable crisis. I paid the price for not being able to stand up to my bosses and say, "This proposal isn't going to happen." I was the one on the ground, and because of that, I took the shrapnel.

A CORPORATE MYTH

Learning from Mistakes

To embark on the journey towards your goals and dreams requires bravery. To remain on that path requires courage. The bridge that merges the two is commitment.

—Steve Maraboli, author

As far as I'm aware, the US Army first used the process of "after-action reviews" with a focus on lessons learned—a great way to internalize improvements and expand abilities. Many companies get input from stakeholders, fill pages of flip charts, and produce wonderful documentation of how they will do better next time. Until they focus on implementing the feedback and lessons learned, all that internal corporate soul-searching turns out to be a complete waste of time.

Two main factors contribute to this lack of follow-through: navel-gazing and an absence of true learning.

NAVEL-GAZING

Many of my clients have spent millions on self-examination, but when asked what they gained, they give no answer because they don't know how to measure the return on investment. They spend too much time looking backward and get paralyzed by their past.

I have attended countless meetings where people spent hours dissecting why something failed. Failure mode analysis works well when *applied properly to construct a new or improved process,* but not as an ongoing, no-end-in-sight exercise, or a "let's check the box and go back to normal," as the next case illustrates.

Brenda knew she had to do something as VP of a defense contractor. When I met her, her team's performance had been plummeting.

Their lackluster results partly reflected misalignment between Brenda and her senior staff. By the time her clear messages about performance expectations seeped through the layers of management, the message had been changed and diluted.

Two issues contributed to this. First, because of her senior team's inability to stop analyzing why they failed, they had unintentionally sabotaged her message: "What can we do to get back on track and succeed?" They had created "failure mode paralysis," which kept them from moving forward and acting. Second, middle management encouraged the frontline to adopt a victim attitude— "this is a tough business"—which demotivated the team.

As I discussed the current state of affairs with Brenda, her keen instincts told her she needed to make some bold moves. She decided on a three-pronged attack: clear accountability, frontline engagement and visibility, and a change in performance culture. Recognizing the connection between leading and encouraging the right organizational behaviors, we agreed on the following three steps to implement her inner philosophy.

Step 1. Call Out Her Senior Team Publicly

At a weekly review of metrics, everyone began to talk in great detail about why they failed again. For example, people had changed due dates without any action plans on how to recover and get back on track. They just whined and resigned themselves to the status quo.

Channeling her toughest "inner leader," Brenda pounded the table and said, "Enough! I don't care how we got here. What are we going to do to get *there*?" [pointing to the target]. "I don't want to hear another 'why' again. I want a plan for moving forward. Period."

This strong emotional response shocked them and stopped them in their tracks. She made it clear that mediocrity would not be acceptable anymore.

Step 2. Go Down to the Shop Floor

Every month, Brenda selected a trade and job and joined that team, crawling and moving around the site while watching the crew execute the work order. This not only increased her knowledge of the work, but also engaged the whole workforce. As a result, they would do anything for her. Instead of "management by walking around," Brenda opted for "management by crawling around and doing."

Step 3. Allow Crews to Take Charge

Brenda would pop in unannounced on weekly crew meetings and employee-led meetings we called boardwalks, and participated fully as a team member. This established an easy, regular interface for her and her managers with the front line.

The result? The team developed a strong alignment for achievement. Performance accelerated, moving the organization to a new level of success. Brenda had successfully transformed their culture, and their major client rewarded them with more work.

People often use failure as an excuse for paralysis and nonaccountability. By taking these three steps, Brenda had shifted that mindset.

ABSENCE OF TRUE LEARNING

If an organization isn't set up to ensure that employees practice and embody any new learning that comes from failure analysis, it often falls by the wayside, impeding success.

Psychometric testing is a common example. It reveals certain characteristics of individuals, usually coded in some form. For instance, during the week after completing a psychometric session, you might go around telling people, "I am a Green with a little bit of Yellow" or "I'm a Follower." But typically, the information and possible benefits fade away because leadership hasn't made those insights a priority. The same holds true for lesson learned sessions and after-action reviews.

We have seen the power of intuition, reflection, and solitude. We have also discovered that behaviors can be changed. Now it is time to look at some of the tools we have to leverage both.

RECAP
Part 2: Creating New Behaviors

1. Seek to understand other people and go to where they are.

2. Move beyond emotions, however intense or thick they might be.

3. Show up differently. Trust depends on presence and action, not on words.

4. Be humble and cultivate the ability to recognize your own errors.

5. Follow up on any commitments that emerge from exercises on risk and failure.

6. Make surprise visits to the team to evaluate and reinforce the commitments that come out of after-action reviews.

7. Spend as much time on implementing the suggested changes from after-action reviews as you do on the reviews themselves.

8. Have champions and assign them the responsibility for executing agreed-upon milestones. Hold people accountable.

9. Invite the senior team to address failures as much as achievements.

10. Be willing to "fall on your sword" in public.

11. Reach out beyond your senior team for one-on-one conversations.

12. Stay open to conversations going in other directions than you expected.

13. Discourage navel-gazing. What you do about failure is far more important than wallowing in it.

14. Make sure you have the right tools in place to consistently evaluate mistakes in real time, as opposed to the once-a-year "how did we get here?" deep dive.

PART 3

OPTIMIZING THE TOOLS OF THE TRADE

You can have all the tools in the world, but if you don't genuinely believe in yourself, it's useless.

—Ken Jeong, comedian

9

ACCESSORIZING WISELY

Optimize Your Top Tools

The challenge of any business owner is not only to keep the saw sharp, but also to know if you even have a need for such a tool.

—Michael E. Gerber, author

Leaders have always had access to a myriad of tools to help accelerate growth and performance. Training, process models, and technology are all available in the outer business world.

For many leaders, throwing money at these "fixes" has been a way of satisfying board members and shareholders by showing the world that they are "doing something"—even if investing in them is more important than actually evaluating their benefits and cost-effectiveness.

Rogue leaders understand the importance of doing inner reflective work *before* investing in any additional help such as tools and processes, something that is a fairly rare occurrence. The importance of setting time aside for reflection to answer these questions and make sure the tools make sense, as discussed in the beginning of the book, cannot be overstated.

Questions to ask yourself: Why should I add this tool to our work environment? What is the measurable benefit? Am I doing this to please my bosses or shareholders? What impact will it have on my organization? How will it be integrated into our workforce? How do they feel about it?

The next four chapters examine the prevalent tools that leaders typically rely on to gain a competitive edge: models, process, technology, and training.

TRAINING AND DEVELOPMENT

Making the Soft Dollar the Hard Dollar

Lifelong learning is a must, and it is up to governments and employees to invest in training and for employees to commit to constantly update their skill set.

—Alain Dehaze, CEO, Adecco Group

For many years, company leaders have looked at training and development as necessary evils, as if to say, "Let me buy a shiny new toy I can show off to my team and shareholders." Education is touted as one of the best investments a company can make. But if that's the case, why isn't it providing the returns we expect?

"Soft dollar" approaches, such as incentives and training tend to generate "soft returns," precisely because that's how we see and categorize them. The hard investments on equipment, new staff, software, all get scrutinized for the impact they make on the bottom line.

Leaders often fail to analyze the impact of soft dollar investments they make. Does the staff use the training? Has the production rate increased as desired? Did the millions spent on corporate culture advance the company in any way?

An example: My granddaughter was recently placed in dance class. Her mom could have checked the box and felt good about putting her in an after-school activity. The real gain though was her growth in social skills, confidence, and creative self. If we just look at the purchase of classes as the outcome, we may miss the true impact, good or bad.

We generally don't look at soft skill investments candidly; instead, we find ways to justify decisions by checking the box or miss the powerful impact we don't see.

Without the proper follow-up and feedback on training and development, most learning goes out the window after a few weeks. The road to stagnant skill development is littered with certificates, workshop binders, and pretty colored diagrams.

When we ask "What ROI did we get for our training?" the response often is "We trained all our people!" not "Here's what they learned and the impact it has had."

We may feel comfortable that we have spent money on our people, but usually that's the end of the story. Embedding new learning requires interactive, sustained follow-up, as well as putting the new knowledge into practice. People are partners. Not assets.

One of my clients, a major oil producer, developed a program to help young professionals step into their new supervisory roles. Given their company culture of command and control, as well as a focus on titles and certificates, classroom work alone was not going to be sufficient. The only way to embed robust leadership development was to combine classwork and workshops with coaching and actual practice in the field every day. That constant feedback loop to their supervisors and the support of their bosses allowed true, sustained development to take place.

As another example of positive soft-side investments, my niece works for Atlassian, an innovative tech company that has created a committed and creative team by purposefully focusing on the "softer side." Employees have access to breakfast and lunch all day, can work from home one day a week, and get shares in the company. Every Friday, they kick off the weekend with a social event. As a result, contributions and ideas happen naturally.

The use of the word "soft" when talking about investing in people is an injustice in my view. Without people, there would be no business or profits. As we will see in chapters ahead, going rogue means understanding that the soft stuff is really the hard stuff. Your people, along with your engagement level with them, are what add value to a company every day.

MODELS IN FASHION

Shortening the Runway

You have to have a business model that you believe in and like.

—Brian L. Roberts, CEO, Comcast

This model. That diagram. This procedure. Many of my clients have extremely complicated management models and operating systems that include all of the above. An operating system (OS) is basically a model of the rules and regulations by which a company will run. It tells the team "this is how we will work day to day."

One client's senior leader held up the OS manual and told the assembled team, "This will save us." Nodding, the crowd felt better that they had the key to going forward. But nothing could have been further from the truth.

Models and manuals are important documents, but they best serve as guidelines. Unless they are impossibly executed to perfection, relying on them *as the solution* can lead to problems and errors.

Many organizations struggle and sometimes collapse trying to create and update detailed models of their business systems. While I encourage using models and acronyms to clarify and simplify, more often than not, employees feel inundated with them.

Models bring order to chaos, but they rarely reflect everyday reality. With clients, I have created hundreds of flowcharts to map out *what really goes on,* and then we use a process map to streamline the flow. You have to first map out what actually happens day to day before you can model how you want it to be. That is the only way for this tool to be effective.

For one client, I showed a process-flow manual to the frontline people who add value every day to the organization and performed a random survey about the OS manual's contents. The supervisors had some idea of what the manual contained, but their team did not.

I also asked how many times the supervisors had used the manual as a reference *before making a decision*, which it was specifically designed to do. Very few had. They didn't make good use of the well-mapped-out pathway detailed in the manual. As a result, their stated path wasn't directly related to what they were actually doing daily.

Models can help us understand the space we need to work in and the steps we need to take to make better decisions. I have found that far too often, team members do not internalize the models designed to be used daily. Yet many office walls are covered with countless displays and reports, filled with arrows and rectangles and bars.

Here is an example: On Mondays, the leadership team for a multinational company got together for an extended meeting to brainstorm ways to ensure a good start to the week. The business model demanded it. Most of the leadership team was in the meeting room until noon and then off to lunch—a total of four hours!

Overlay that with hundreds of pending emails for them to answer, calculations to perform, and administrative tasks to address, and the leadership team was basically starting their week at 1 pm after lunch. The model for effective management soon broke down as leaders were absent from their teams a half day to start the week. There was constant catch-up after that. The model was driving a chaotic business flow.

Models and maps are useful guides, but they should never be a substitute for the actual journey. Challenges emerge every day that require decisions. Let the model be a framework that keeps you on track for the big picture, but don't rely on it as a solution in and of itself.

PROCESS TOOLS AND SIRENS

Avoid Crashing Against the Shore

There's always a siren, singing you to shipwreck. Some of us may be more susceptible than others are, but there's always a siren. It may be with us all our lives, or it may be many years or decades before we find it or it finds us. But when it does find us, if we're lucky, we're Odysseus tied up to the ship's mast, hearing the song with perfect clarity, but ferried to safety by a crew whose ears have been plugged with beeswax. If we're not at all lucky, we're another sort of sailor stepping off the deck to drown in the sea.

—Caitlín R. Kiernan, author, *The Drowning Girl*

L eaders at all levels rely on models and processes to help their organizations execute objectives, but this collection of well-worn management choices can become a big "leadership pacifier"—a comfort blanket they often reach for. Though familiar, it might serve only to keep leaders from coming up with a more effective response.

When they use these tools exclusively to solve every issue—even those involving human relations—they are asking for trouble. Putting too much trust in processes can even be dangerous. But the sirens of modern technology keep beckoning, and leaders keep crashing against the shores.

Processes or tools made by humans have to be used by humans—and sometimes the unpredictable human element can lead to problems.

Here are some real-life examples of "crashing against the shore" and how to avoid the otherwise inevitable.

CASE STUDY: SIX SIGMA BLACK BELTS

Six Sigma—a set of certifiable techniques and tools for process improvement—can help many businesses. For one of my clients, it was their core approach, at least on the surface. They had invested hundreds of thousands of dollars in what's known as Lean/Six Sigma training and development.

As a matter of fact, the entire senior leadership team had achieved Six Sigma "black-belt" status, and the general workforce had "green belt" certification. The senior leader was convinced that this training would give them an edge in the marketplace.

Though developing your people to hedge your bets is all good, certification does not guarantee successful implementation. If managers and leaders evaluate the ROI on training in terms of certification alone, they can get the false impression that they have now done enough—one of the hidden dangers.

At the client site, the tools were in place and a Six Sigma coach was even there. But that didn't guarantee anything, because despite having the tools, the people looked for workarounds, not fully embracing their new skills as Six Sigma Green Belts. As a result, being a Six Sigma organization didn't translate into high performance.

Not all was lost. Many of the integrated product teams (IPTs), utilizing their Six Sigma foundation, chose a different path and achieved a higher level of success—and it all had to do with how people managed their business and the way they executed their daily tasks.

The company operated as "cross-functional," meaning they organized their work around function instead of product. Companies that do this rather than focusing on budget or product viability typically face challenges. In principle, functions such as software and hardware engineering lend their expertise to their internal client/product.

In this particular case, functions charged the various product teams according to time, but no one took responsibility for the health of the product or project, so schedules suffered and costs increased.

The project managers managed the functions by creating a common goal within the IPTs for schedule and cost. These teams actually reflected a more collaborative environment than what the organization created under Six Sigma.

Overwhelmingly, the organization's culture remained more or less the same. And although the specific programs we worked on continued to flourish, the overall business wasn't moving forward fast enough.

None of the processes will solve anything unless the culture uses them to maximum potential. In this client's case, the company culture exalted the presence of Six Sigma tools, but not their daily implementation.

PROCESS FATIGUE

A major oil producer serves as another example of what can happen to an organization when it encounters what I call "process fatigue."

The client had a process safety handbook touted as the way to move forward. And although everyone had a copy of the manual, the frontline people didn't really understand it or effectively execute it. To improve the situation, the leadership team decided to rework the handbook to include everyday real-life moments. By matching the words on the page to actual operational issues, they created alignment.

Many companies put a lot of time and energy into these handbooks, which then just sit in desk drawers collecting dust.

Let me be really clear: The process will not save you. The tools will not save you. But the people around you can save the organization—depending on how you lead them:

> The intentions of a tool are what it does. A hammer intends to strike, a vise intends to hold fast, a lever intends to lift. They are what it is made for. But

sometimes a tool may have other uses that you don't know. Sometimes in doing what you intend, you also do what the knife intends, without knowing.

—Philip Pullman, author, His Dark Materials Trilogy: The Golden Compass / The Subtle Knife / The Amber Spyglass

Another siren also calls, the loudest siren of all: the siren of technology . . .

SOLVING THE TECHNOLOGY TRAP

Gaining the Advantage

Technology is a useful servant but a dangerous master.

—Christian Lous Lange, historian

The fast pace of technology demands an agile and responsive presence. Technology today advances in months or weeks, rather than the years it used to take. Early adopters need to update every three months or so just to stay ahead. And although rapid technological advances can be easily seen, some important changes remain unseen: as people strive to adapt and learn new behaviors, neural patterns in their brains also change and develop.

Due to the widespread use of sophisticated digital tech, we now expect to get instant, even live, feedback. For example, if you need specific data on something, search Google or ask Siri or Alexa to get what you need in seconds.

The same goes for communication in both our business and our personal lives. Not so long ago, if we didn't hear from our best friend or loved one all day, we didn't worry, because we knew we could connect with them face-to-face in a matter of hours or a few days.

Nowadays, however, if you don't respond via email or text immediately, people think something is up, something is wrong: "OMG. You didn't respond to my Facebook post. You didn't answer me on my Snapchat. Are you okay? I haven't heard from you in twenty-five minutes."

Imagine a millennial time traveler going back to the days of the Pony Express—waiting days, weeks, or even months for a reply to a letter. Forget it. Now we expect everything to happen at hyper speed, wanting data and information to process ever faster. Conditioned to expect faster and faster responses, we rush to make decisions, often making mistakes and errors of judgment. Our brains cannot handle the amount and speed of information, leading to fatigue and stress.

Complicating the matter is the lack of experience and know-how as the world shifts toward a "techno-literate" skill set. It can be a tough road for many leaders who need to understand how to unleash technology's potential but don't have the time or inclination to become an expert.

According to Annelie Gullström, a global expert in digital transformation and tech innovator, "A lot of leaders are scared to admit they don't understand IoT, AI, VR, AR, big Data, block chain. It is much easier to say no to a new proposed initiative internally and stick to the traditional that is familiar."

Members of the workforce are often in the forefront of new technology, and like their clients, they demand change. Annelie confirms, "The risk is that the firm will do only scattered digital initiatives to please the board, but they will not drive change and adapt the organization accordingly and work smarter. Studies show that firms that focus on both digital customer experience and digital operational excellence are up to 26% more profitable."

But the key here is the right technology—and the right response.

Conditioned now to expect immediate responses, we tend to lose focus. Too often, we believe we have answered the call, but we don't ask the really important question: Did we respond *correctly*?

Many of my clients have invested millions in software, hardware, apps, and other digital processes and then don't understand why they don't get a return—or, worse, they don't take full advantage of the technology they've purchased.

Managing technology and data is critical. It's all about understanding its potential, keeping current, and then ensuring a meaningful response. Don't run from it in fear, nor run toward it blindly as a panacea.

Managing the overall pace of change is a whole other matter.

RECAP
Part 3: Optimizing the Tools of the Trade

Before you invest in a process, model, or technology, ask yourself the following:

1. What proof do I have that it will do what it says?

2. Do I really need it? Is it a "nice to have" or a "need to have"?

3. What do my current systems, gadgets, and software provide now?

4. What does my team use?

5. What feedback do my team members give? Don't ask if they want the latest software, because they will almost always say yes—our minds love new things.

6. What uses will we get from this?

7. Do I have the budget and resources to make sure everyone gets trained and feels comfortable adopting the new process or technology?

8. What is the true cost of implementation?

9. Who will pay for it?

10. Have we gotten enough value from previous purchases?

PART 4

MANAGING CHANGE ROGUE-STYLE

Without change there is no innovation, creativity, or incentive for improvement. Those who initiate change will have a better opportunity to manage the change that is inevitable.

—William Pollard, clergyman

CREATING CHANGE

Knowing When to Shift Gears

The illiterate of the twenty-first century will not be those who cannot read and write, but those who cannot learn, unlearn, and relearn.

—Alvin Toffler, author

How do we know when we need to change? At the very least, companies need to change to keep pace with their competition. It's better, of course, to outpace the competition.

From a leadership viewpoint, shifting gears can often propel a company ahead of competitors. Your actions change the rules, forcing followers to behave in ways they wouldn't have considered. Radical change can induce agility and growth, helping innovators stay ahead of the curve *by being the curve*—or it can just create chaos.

Change drives progress, but it must be done purposefully. Keep in mind, though, that such change tends to benefit the disruptor rather than the disrupted.

Some would argue that you must change all the time to keep pace, almost like the cost-of-living index for inflation. I disagree.

Perpetual change does not allow for a rhythm to be established or a foundation to be laid. The core of your business must be well defined and constant to build trust and confidence in your clients and customers, as well as employees.

There are known triggers for change that will let you know when to consider taking action. Some examples, although not inclusive:

1. Internal triggers (inside the organization): testing of new services and products, employee discord, misalignment, lack of values, vision and mission off track, unwanted behaviors, performance gaps, introduction of new technologies and processes.

2. External triggers: market change, competition, catastrophic event, demand by shareholders, succession of governance, new laws.

In the chapters that follow, we will look in depth at internal and external triggers and the best ways to handle change.

DISRUPTING DISRUPTION

Going Rogue on Yourself

Undermine their pompous authority, reject their moral standards, make anarchy and disorder your trademarks, cause as much chaos and disruption as possible but don't let them take you ALIVE.

—Sid Vicious, the Sex Pistols

One of my colleagues said, "If I hear the word 'disruption' one more time, I am going to disrupt somebody's face." I believe it will soon go the way of others, such as "agile," and, my personal all-time favorites, "synergy" and "alignment." Provided we don't overuse them, these words can still be still effective.

I will use "disruption" here, as anything that disturbs the status quo—especially in the marketplace. Disruption creates a different stimulus and adds new energy into the system, creating the conditions for significant change.

At its core, disruption introduces something different into the organizational or industry equation. Metaphorically, we might say it changes the "energy field" and opens up a potentially infinite array of new applications.

There is always going to be external change. That being said, we can choose be the disruptor and trigger change. To be optimally effective, that change needs to be introduced in a purposeful, strategic way.

Here are some real-life examples of internal driven disruptive change.

Good leaders direct the collective energy of their workforce or group, guiding and reshaping it according to feedback—always focusing on reaching their objectives. Even the best leaders in the world need assistance from their teams—they never achieve success by themselves.

As a leader, you have the seldom-used ability to accelerate reshaping and reforming your culture or your path. Sometimes the landscape needs to be boldly shaken up in ways that that will create new experiences and therefore new neural pathways.

This means taking some *action* involving physical movement that helps rewire neurons and open new pathways for learning. This applies to teams as well as to individuals. The act itself creates change.

Example 1. Shake Things Up

My client was complaining that her team wasn't focused during their weekly review of the business and action planning. She was frustrated that she had to do everything for them. And they were not adding value. I proposed "Let them run the meeting in rotation."

She said, "They won't be able to handle it."

When she announced that Fred was going to run the meeting, the response was shock, dismay, and backpedaling. It was an ugly meeting for Fred but you can be sure people were focused and scrambling to show up well. After four meetings, everything ran like clockwork, and her team loved it. The energy had shifted and the meeting became robust.

Example 2. Give Space and Trust: The Case of the Willing Hillbilly

When I first saw John, a manufacturing supervisor, talk with his crew on a large defense construction program, I was surprised. During his talk, most of his crew looked away, did other distracting things, or turned their backs on him.

A wily character, John prided himself on playing a dumb hillbilly from West Virginia. He was anything but—just a joker at heart.

I asked him how his crew meetings went, and he confided that they weren't going well. He also said he'd like to make them better. The crew briefing agenda contained only some weekly announcements, some morale boosters, and a section on safety compliance.

I suggested to John that he talk with a few influencers on the team to find out what they would like to see. After all, they functioned as his internal clients. Many of them wanted to know about their performance but were afraid the numbers would be used as a weapon against them, as they had in the past.

John and I had agreed to meet in a week to go over preparations for the agenda and practice showing the team their performance numbers. The next day, John called me and said, "I'm having my meeting today in an hour. Please come."

I sensed impending doom. John had written the agenda and the performance numbers on a piece of cardboard and used a flip chart to draw details by hand. I thought, *this crew talk spells disaster.*

It didn't. Although John's presentation wasn't perfect, I could see his team was curious about this new approach. Not all, but more than before. For the first time, he talked about their shared performance and recognized their good work that week. He asked them to solve gaps together, instead of castigating them. Something had changed.

No one said so, but I knew that his talk inspired and triggered his team to change direction. So much so, in fact, that the president of the shipyard came by and asked to see what John was doing and how he did it. Word spread quickly, followed by a visit from the VP for his area.

Soon, every one of his colleagues asked if they could attend his meetings. Over time, he refined these gatherings into powerful meetings. He invited more dialogue, the crew consistently knew their performance numbers, and eventually his team took over leading the meeting. His success depended on taking that first step: holding that meeting—which even I was skeptical of. He had effectively jumped into the pool and worried about his swimming strokes later.

I learned a lesson that day: Let your employees set the pace, as risky as that might seem at first. Give them space, and then help them fill it well. On reflection, I'm glad I decided not to challenge him about whether he was ready to "jump." Clearly, the time had arrived for him to do something different.

THE MIND-BODY CONNECTION

A Unique Way to Drive Change

The mind shapes the body, and the body shapes the mind.

—Amy Cuddy, author

My mom worked as a Feldenkrais practitioner, and according to the basic philosophy of this mind-body healing approach, we can relearn and create new neural pathways through specially designed body movements. Remarkable transformations can take place, such as being able to see or walk again. It works both ways: new behaviors lay down new nerve pathways, and new neural pathways enable us to change behavior and do something different.

I saw this during my time in the neuro-trauma unit where people made some remarkable physical and mental transformations after severe injuries. Numerous stories exist about talking to people in a coma, and how those talks stimulated the patient's neural activity, eventually helping them recover.

My own experience confirms that. After a freak accident, Barry had fallen into a severe coma and, as a quadriplegic, would likely never walk again. As his aides, my colleague John and I decided to keep talking to him every time we saw him, bathed him, or moved him. We focused on normal conversation, which included jokes and news of the day.

One day, as we carried him to the bathing area, I had my hands on his buttocks. John leaned over and said, "Barry, I wouldn't let Paul touch me there." Barry broke into a smile. The three of us laughed, and from that moment, his consciousness began to return. Barry wasn't a lost patient. If we had labeled him as such, he might not have come out of the coma. The energy John and I spent on Barry did finally create a different body state and neural response.

Nothing ever remains static. It may appear so, but it isn't. We always have an opportunity to execute differently.

The same kind of rerouting can happen with groups. Because of conditioning and socialization, most teams respond to old patterns the same way over and over again. To change that, we must focus on incoming stimuli and pay close attention to how we respond.

One of the most powerful ways to create new behavior is through experiential learning, which connects the mind and the body. Classic books such as *The Inner Game of Tennis* (Random House, 1997) show clearly that we can accelerate learning not by absorbing more content, but by teaching new skills through *the experience* of it.

How can leaders use the mind-body connection to help retrain teams to respond and behave in more effective and meaningful ways? How can we break up old patterns and replace them?

The following story illustrates how.

My client leader asked us all to do a high-altitude obstacle course. Those of us afraid of heights were to go last so we could watch and learn. I was the last one through and had one more station to go when I flipped on the wire and found myself dangling upside down ten stories in the air. It was the scariest moment in my life. I feel nauseated just writing about it here.

I found a way through. It wasn't perfect execution at all, but that didn't matter. What mattered is that by taking this new action, we began to develop trust and respect for one another as well as confidence to face the challenges ahead. We had a new focus and energy.

$$\left(17 \right)$$

REWIRING COMPLACENCY FOR GROWTH

Taking Away the Pacifier

Because of the power of neuroplasticity, you can, in fact, reframe your world and rewire your brain so that you are more objective. You have the power to see things as they are so that you can respond thoughtfully, deliberately, and effectively to everything you experience.

—Elizabeth Thornton, author

Good managers take time to ensure that everyone on their team feels content—but not complacent. Complacency stifles growth in performance. People will not give additional time, energy, and creativity if there is no incentive to do so.

As we have explored previously, a sense of pressure accelerates change and growth. We all know the often-used motivational poster of a seed pushing through the soil as it grows. Soil alone won't work. You also need some fertilizer, sunshine, air, and water.

One of the maintenance managers at a large chemical plant had scheduled regular morning meetings with his work group, but all they did was discuss the previous night's updates and review risks. It was a complacent passive meeting with low participation.

The manager wanted his employees to focus on specific meaningful actions, not just use the meetings for status updates. He began to ask his team to focus on the numbers that documented their success or failure and take action. This tangible spotlight made them initially uncomfortable.

By introducing a new set of Key Performance indicators (KPIs) and asking the team to understand and review them in the meeting, the executive helped them think about success in a more tangible way and brought clarity to the actions they took to sustain it.

The leader demanded not just the performance numbers, *but the context behind* the data results from his senior staff.

Intuitive leadership operates on the principle that keeping your team uncomfortable stimulates energy and innovation. By contrast, complacency and routine drive inefficiency.

If the world changes rapidly and your team does not keep pace, you end up falling behind. Forcing your managers and leaders to get out of their comfort zone can create growth, insight, and innovation.

Here are eleven ideas to keep your team on a path of growth:

1. Challenge Them

Mix it up and give them assignments that stretch them. Push them to work with others they haven't worked with before. Give them the space to innovate.

2. Encourage No-Fault Creativity

If I know I have permission to try some things that may not work out, I will be more likely to take action based on my best knowledge and analysis. Having a framework for cultivating new ideas can make a big difference. Incubate them in small batches, and then roll them out after doing beta tests. Chapter 18 on stealth change management covers much the same principle. Start small—you don't need everyone, just a critical mass. Create a space for your workforce to push back or to design new methods.

3. Demonstrate Conscience and Affinity Leadership

Humans have evolved to lay blame as well as to understand what happened. Risk-averse organizations tend to stifle action—especially innovative action—for fear of failure and blame. Naturally, this creates problems for the organization. Every team needs to have a voice willing to speak up against the status quo and point out potential risks and bad decisions. Rogue leaders should identify and encourage these voices; letting them know that space is safe.

4. Be Willing to Hear Other Voices

We all have heard about Abraham Lincoln staffing his cabinet with his enemies. Why? To ensure that the best thinking would emerge, and that every action would be thoroughly examined without prejudice.

Avoid filling your team with like-minded people—it is much better to have a diverse team. We naturally tend to surround ourselves with "like frequencies," but we also need to make sure that other voices get heard.

5. Short-Circuiting the Status Quo: Change Your Tune

As we have seen previously, by sending a different impulse, or message, down your team's neural pathways, you can begin to reconfigure brain connections as you see fit. Otherwise, without change, the responses would be the same. You and your organization would march along as you always have, likely missing opportunities to drive the organization.

Ray had just started as the new station manager of a major airline business unit, the result of a merger. As such, the staff perceived him as an outsider. The workforce assumed he had no affinity or empathy for the challenges they faced. Even though he promised visibility and accessibility, months later those words seemed hollow.

Their perception did not fully fit the facts, but it reflected something he needed to pay attention to. In other words, what he regarded as effective did not land in the way he wished or intended.

As a leader, Ray had two options: continue to be frustrated that his message wasn't coming across or change how he delivered it. He looked for other ways to show up, including hanging out on the shop floor, participating in meetings, being more accessible, and showing that he cared. It helped him create a successful environment and an aligned team.

Changing the narrative takes time and effort, but it is an effective tool. Too often, though, leaders throw up their hands and do nothing but complain.

6. Channel Your Tantrum:
Do Things Boldly and Differently

This technique needs to be used sparingly and purposefully. Using a controlled tantrum can get attention and, more important, can disrupt and open up the team to move in a different direction.

This occurred as I began a new project working with a managing director. A few months into it, progress remained slow. We couldn't figure out why his senior team still strongly resisted my presence and working with me on the project plan. Leaders put off meetings and commitments, and, as a result, missed important milestones.

How could we reflect this back to the team without it sounding like a lecture? Yet we needed to grab their attention and encourage commitment and a sense of ownership.

With a twinkle in his eyes, the managing director laid out a plan. He set up a meeting with his team and opened with the following question: "Why aren't we making progress as a team on this project?"

"Paul needs to do more."

"Ask Paul."

"I'm surprised he is moving so slow. It's his project."

Once everyone was done, and the bait taken, the managing director slammed his fist on the table, something he would normally never do. This shocked his team. Having their complete attention, he let them know this was *their* factory and *their* responsibility, and *they* had to own it. He then asked me to leave the room. I don't know what he said, but it worked as a major turning point—from then on, the team's effectiveness improved (as did our relationship).

7. Play Musical Chairs

A senior executive I worked with observed that one of his distracted team members always sat in the same place during meetings and spent most of the time on his computer answering emails or playing on social media. One morning, the executive showed up early and sat in the chair where his distracted team member usually sat, forcing the guy to find a chair up front where he couldn't hide. This created sufficient dissonance to break the pattern, all due to changing one small thing.

8. Stretch: Assign Tasks to People Beyond Their Normal Responsibility

Every now and then, using normal channels and those responsible for managing them may not be the best approach—especially if "normal" gets you stuck.

In a large petrochemical plant, the senior team faced a multi-million-dollar expansion, as well as a shutdown of the plant. This had to be meticulously planned. Lost days would cost millions.

The manager wisely decided to assign much of the planning and scheduling of the event to the number-two guy, who normally just managed the master schedule. By linking the master scheduler to the contractors, that interface was more responsive and robust. With the right people partnering, he helped create an executable plan and schedule and integrated the team's efforts for reaching the final objective: a safe and efficient turnaround.

9. Always Surprise

Doug Leard, the leader in my first consulting and coaching firm, drove home this point. His team was spread all over the globe, engaged in different projects, and Doug wanted to bring everyone together in a more productive way. Because we all worked in different locations, he knew he needed to build bonds of trust, as well as a commitment to excellence.

At a quarterly retreat in San Francisco, we spent many hours preparing for an eight-hour meeting about our consulting projects and then turned in our summaries. One by one, we would be covering thirteen current projects.

Doug welcomed us all: "Sometimes you have to follow, and sometimes you have to lead. You have all done a great job preparing for today's meeting, and your summaries will be available at the end of the day for everyone to take with them. Let's play ball!"

With that, he opened up a bag and tossed out San Francisco Giants baseball caps for all of us, and off we went to the baseball game that afternoon.

We had a great time and also caught up on each other's work. Doug knew he was building something more powerful that would keep us motivated and committed day to day. As a result, we all felt part of a team larger than ourselves.

10. Hold People Accountability: Purposeful Disruption

In a large-scale naval construction company, the engineering group occupied a position near the top of the employee totem pole. Though the group included some of the best and the brightest, their work had almost no visibility because of the long lead times. Often, it could take three to five years between creating the designs and actually implementing them as part of a naval vessel.

Greg's senior engineering team started out on a new design and fell behind schedule almost immediately. Slippage in the early days didn't seem like much to be concerned about, but it could become a wave of pending work many times greater by the time they reached the construction completion date.

Monday morning progress meetings were challenging, even painful. Each manager went through his committed milestones for the next two weeks. Sometimes they lasted two hours but were filled with nothing more than back-and-forth comments such as "that date is good," "hold that date," "need to move it two weeks." In other words, the meetings amounted to nothing more than a status update.

When I asked Greg if he could tell me the purpose of the meeting, he said he wanted everyone from his "brain trust" to meet in the same room to manage their progress. I then asked him what management decisions they had collectively made. "Very little," he admitted.

I suggested that they could simply go online and mail in their reports. We spoke about how he wanted accountability and focus, but he hadn't communicated those elements—instead, he was letting the team off the hook. Greg decided to be bold and change the way he asked questions in the meeting.

The first time he did so, it shocked the team. He announced that if they had met their deadline, they did not need to report it. With that change alone, he saved valuable time, and everyone looked happy, nodding at the new change.

But when he asked them to move some milestone date two weeks earlier and explained that he wanted a tangible plan to get back on schedule, they did not respond so enthusiastically. The room fell quiet.

The team had fallen into a routine of updating status, but not being held accountable for schedule slippage or corrective action. Greg's initial line of questioning took his team by surprise. The result: halfhearted responses and excuses. I could feel the tension in the room.

Greg later voiced his concern that this approach would not work. I acknowledged his frustration and fears. We both agreed that the next meeting would be critical. If he capitulated and went back to the default of status updates, he would never get his team on track.

The following Monday, Greg's team began to test him again with status updates. After the first two managers tried and failed, the group smartly picked up those cues. By the third Monday, the meeting reflected more accountability, better dates, and commitments to action.

By changing accountability and the line of questioning, Greg slowly changed his team's behavior and long-term performance. They were able to get back on schedule.

11. Trigger Significant Emotional Events

Sometimes drawing a line in the sand to mark a decisive change challenges the status quo and, especially if unexpected, can trigger emotional reactions like shock and panic. Such abrupt changes need to be well planned to avoid unwelcome surprises.

An example from my university days illustrates what I mean. At final test time, one of my professors fired a starter gun as we were not paying attention, talking over him, and being boisterous. It was a significant emotional event, as he berated us in a way never heard before. He lost his cool, to reestablish control.

The examples above show how leaders can interrupt established neural pathways and behaviors and change the responses of their teams and organizations. They all share a common factor: introducing an experiential shock or change to the system that shifts accepted norms, prompting people to stop and think, *Wait a minute! This is new and not what I expected.*

Our minds will always gravitate to something new, even though our past responses may be deeply conditioned through repetition.

STEALTH CHANGE MANAGEMENT

People don't resist change. They resist being changed!

—Peter Senge, author

For many leaders, managing change is a struggle in its execution. Many of my clients have spent countless hours and money, investing their people's time in a big rollout of the latest initiative—involving countless all-company meetings, town-hall gatherings, slogans, and speeches. The circus has truly come to town. And despite all the flipcharts documenting novel ideas, in the end most of them go back to normal and nothing really changes.

Why isn't there even "a flavor of the month" reaction? Because companies do not manage their change rollouts properly. In fact, these are probably the worst ways to manage culture change. Most studies reveal that 70 percent of all change initiatives fail.

So, what to do? Intuitive leadership tells us to go against the grain.

John Kurz, a visionary leader at a large oil firm, has the answer. How does a living body transform? As we all know, the body constantly replaces old cells with new cells. But change or growth doesn't happen all at once. You don't suddenly leave childhood and enter puberty or change from an adolescent into an adult man or a woman. It happens by degrees, small changes at a time. If growth happened too quickly, your body would revolt.

John and other leaders I have worked with understand that sweeping changes almost never stick, but small steps over time can effectively change the culture without generating resistance, overwhelm, or apathy.

It is as if management declared "Let's be "X," and then everyone feels disappointed when the organization doesn't become X. Transforming culture happens in two ways: either a crisis forces change (an external trigger like a market disruption) or leaders make a focused effort to do bring about the desired change (internal trigger).

Change can happen without everyone jumping on the bandwagon. In biology, in fact, very few cells drive changes in metabolism and health. If important metabolic change can occur in our bodies with just a few "change-agent" cells, why not also in organizations?

> Molecular biology has shown that even the simplest of all living systems on earth today, bacterial cells, are exceedingly complex objects. Although the tiniest bacterial cells are incredibly small, weighing less than 10^{-12} gms, each is in effect a veritable micro-miniaturized factory containing thousands of exquisitely designed pieces of intricate molecular machinery, made up altogether of one hundred thousand million atoms, far more complicated than any machine

built by man and absolutely without parallel in the nonliving world.

—**Michael Denton, author,**
Evolution: A Theory in Crisis

Working on a typewriter by touch, like riding a bicycle or strolling on a path, is best done by not giving it a glancing thought. Once you do, your fingers fumble and hit the wrong keys. To do things involving practiced skills, you need to turn loose the systems of muscles and nerves responsible for each maneuver, place them on their own, and stay out of it.

—**Lewis Thomas, author,** ***The Lives of a Cell:***
Notes of a Biology Watcher

We can apply that same apparently radical, but normal thought process here. By taking things slow and quietly, in baby steps, without grand announcements and proclamations, leaders can make significant change without anyone noticing. I call it "stealth change."

Stealth transformation does not mean bad intent. Wise leaders use it to avoid resistance, demotivation due to lack of progress that big initiatives often create. Forget all the fancy balloons and donuts—and simply *act without fanfare.*

John succeeded in shifting his organization from being just safety-focused to being risk-focused as well. He didn't turn a blind eye to safety, but he realized that by carefully managing risk, he and his team would create a more committed and safer workplace.

John understood that not everyone has to go "Yeah!"—that the energy required to get everyone on board will not necessarily continue.

As the company moves forward to launch the latest new thing, it can generate great enthusiasm. That's how our minds work. Then, over time, the excitement runs its course. Too much, and too rapid, change can disorient and exhaust your team, increasing the likelihood they will resist the change—hence, the value of *stealth* change.

As we have seen over the last few chapters, there are a variety of things we can do to drive change internally. But what happens when outside events force us to change?

CRISIS MANAGEMENT
Taking Off Leadership Handcuffs

There cannot be a crisis next week. My schedule is full already.

—Henry Kissinger, former Secretary of State

Like anything in life, a single moment can change everything. What you once thought impossible actually happens. Something you thought you would never experience suddenly shows up.

When you're faced with challenges or opportunities to innovate, "going against the grain"—a core principle of this book—often liberates previously untapped power.

One morning you wake up, your partner has left, and you find yourself alone. All your shared plans have gone up in smoke. As the day goes on, your pulse rate goes way up, and you now consider what once seemed forbidden or impossible: You begin to hear rumblings of your basic instincts and wonder what it would be like to follow your impulse and do things you never did before.

Peter, the manager at a large forestry products plant, woke up one morning in early spring to find he had lost 30 percent of his market overnight due to plummeting prices in Asia.

Later that morning, the chairman of the board of directors called to inform him that if the plant didn't finish at break-even by the end of the year, they would likely close the plant until further notice. He had six months.

In any crisis, you have options: You can think and act reactively for the short term and try to put out the fire. Or you can choose to leverage the crisis and drive for long-term changes that increase performance.

Peter called me in to discuss a possible strategy before the rest of the team got involved. The consequences of not getting it right were obvious. Peter insisted that we take whatever action we needed to meet the board's challenge, refusing to be a victim.

His team had to commit to doing things they hadn't done before. Because the team had no precedent for the new approach, the uncertainty they faced seemed like a thousand shades of gray. On a gut level, Peter knew they had to be bold: Be open to thinking without judgment, use their creativity, and take complete ownership of any unexpected consequences. It would require truly trusting one another.

To drive profitability, the senior team decided to take away any constraints they had previously put on themselves. For example:

1. **Link the front line to the business.** No one could be on the sidelines as they developed the recovery plan.

At small group meetings, everyone heard firsthand about the business environment.

2. **Simplify the message and change the language.** Management-speak wouldn't work with the front line, many of whom had only an eighth-grade education. The plant manager met with the remaining team every week, and he changed the weekly revenue target to "number of logging trucks," which they all understood: "How many logging trucks did we generate this week?"

3. **Work with contractors as full team members.** Peter included all remaining contractors as full members of the team. He did not have time to repeat instructions or hold weekly business reviews.

4. **Show compassion.** He handled any layoffs with upmost care and dignity, along with full union support and family outreach. He also set up assistance for job hunting and additional financial support to help with the transition— no burned bridges.

5. **Open up communication.** He insisted that communication should flow freely up and down the org chart, and that managers would listen to all stakeholders at all levels. Managers stayed out of their offices, and "lived" on the shop floor.

6. **Base all decisions and actions on agreed-upon priorities.** By sharpening focus and using tough triage, he and his team restricted actions to whatever would add value to the balance sheet. Everything else went on hold.

7. **Increase the business review cycle.** Instead of relying on standard weekly and monthly reports, the combined

team took the pulse of the business daily, which drove more effective decision-making that involved input from the front line.

8. **Have more fun, not less.** While this might seem counterintuitive, Peter made sure that his people shared more dinners, participated in community events, and spent time together to reduce stress.

They finished the year at $250,000 above break-even. The plant stayed open and remains a healthy business to this day. Many of the people he had laid off eventually rejoined the team.

They continued to use the successful more open and unrestrained strategy even when they achieved their objectives.

Most of the time, leaders don't have to deal with crisis. They have to effectively manage the day to day. More disconcerting, some act as if everything is a crisis, and as such, put their performance and teams in peril unwittingly.

20

EFFECTIVE TRIAGE

Not Everything Is a Crisis

The term "triage" normally means deciding who gets attention first.

—Bill Dedman, journalist

O ften in high pressure work environments, external inputs are responded to with equal energy and attention. Suddenly, everything is a priority and a crisis, and is met with intense action and activity.

Many leaders initiate action and allow resources to be utilized without really understanding that they can control the company's input as well as its output. Wise leaders ask, "Do we really want to do this?"

An example: One client, who believed in open access, allowed anyone to initiate a complex document known as an engineering change notice request. The change notice needed to be evaluated, processed, and given a thumbs-up or thumbs-down, generating many work-hours by the engineering team.

The result was a system clogged with too many requests. Some of them were critical. There was not enough staff time to handle them, which meant delays, and the important requests were mixed in with the less important.

Once a leader decides to move forward without triage, it can cost a lot more to undo it; it is much better and cost-effective to stop the process before you reach the point of no return. Once again, it goes back to priorities and simplification.

Good triage questions to consider:

1. How does this (issue, project, challenge) fit into our overall priorities?
2. What is the risk if we don't address it?
3. Can we address it a week or a month from now when we have freed up resources?
4. If we take it on, who would be responsible?
5. What does assigning someone do to the person, team, and workload?
6. How does it affect our stakeholders?
7. What additional resources do we need?
8. What potential gains can we expect?
9. What could go wrong?

Triage must be done rapidly, and that means no twelve-hour-long exercises. Instead, ask these questions quickly, and then make your decision to move forward on the issue at hand, forget about it, or postpone it.

In the previous chapters, we have seen that there is so much more under a leader's control internally to drive and manage change. That knowledge and skill set also helps us when external factors demand a response. Another powerful skill that we can harness, and have more control of then we think, is our presence.

RECAP
Part 4: Managing Change Rogue-Style

1. Use movement or action to establish new neural pathways.

2. Jump-start changes in behavior by taking actions that change brain patterns.

3. Take different, purposeful actions that create significant emotional events to "wake up people" and change behaviors and accountability.

4. Turn to shock value to shift behaviors, but use it sparingly.

5. Introduce something new to engage and refocus everyone's mind.

6. Trust and respect one another and don't rely on power by title.

7. Pay attention to the front line at all times.

8. Make the time for inner work and reflection (the leader).

9. Change neural pathways by doing things differently and creating new experiences.

10. Don't wait for a crisis. It can do a lot to sharpen focus, but don't wait for one.

11. Focus on long-term career development and not on training only.

12. Initiate change over time through consistent "stealth" execution; avoid fanfare.

PART 5

SHOWING UP WITH PURPOSE

"Be in" is all about passion. Life is short. There are so many interesting things we can do in our life, and I feel like if someone is just kind of showing up, it's not worth it for them or for us.

—Brad Garlinghouse, CEO

STAND-UP LEADERSHIP

How to Bring Down the House

When you are doing stand-up comedy, you are the writer, producer, director, sometimes bouncer.

—Dane Cook, comic

Picture yourself in a comedy club filled with people drinking, laughing, and talking. The microphone stand glints in the spotlight as the audience waits for the comics to come on stage—collectively, the audience hums with an attitude: "make me laugh." All share a common purpose: they came to be entertained, united in varying degrees of defiance and sobriety.

The late great comic Dick Gregory was once asked in the early '60s how, as a black man, he could perform in all-white clubs. He did so by making fun of himself first. Self-deprecation gave him permission to then turn his sights on others. By channeling the energy toward himself first, he changed the dynamic in the room.

What does any of this have to do with business?

We can look at the arc of a stand-up show's thirty-minute set as an accelerated "rogue life cycle" in business. Comedians must perform reflective work in real time and respond to immediate feedback. Their approach can work as effectively in everyday business life as it does on stage.

My family hails from the world of improvisation and comedy. My mother loved her work as an improvisational actress; my sister-in-law, actress Suzanne Kent, a founding member of the famed Groundlings Theater in LA, the birthplace of comedy giants such as Phil Hartman, Will Ferrell, and Melissa McCarthy. In our twenties, my brother, David, and I had a national touring improv group, and he also enjoyed being a member of the Groundlings Sunday Show.

As a comic, I have used tricks to ensure I had a good shot at having a good evening. Note the key phrase "have a shot." Any comic who says he or she has never bombed has never been on stage. Nothing is guaranteed—especially when you have to improvise (this also applies in business). Here are my top five tricks and techniques.

1. Quietly Observe and Go Inward

Over the years in stand-up, I noticed that many comics would stay backstage or drink at the bar. At first, this surprised me, but later I realized that the more successful comics used that time to read the audience. I used to do that too as an emcee. I would watch the crowd and the way they behaved collectively, making a mental note of who might be trouble or agitated, who was in a good mood, and who was there for cheap beer.

Many comics missed this opportunity because they were too self-absorbed: "My material. My routine." I found it shocking. This is critical reflective time.

New and seasoned leaders alike would be wise to spend time with their teams—not to talk but to listen, watch, and observe how their teams, perform, feel, and react. The more mindfulness and attention you bring to this, the more information you can glean on gaps you can close and issues that may hinder reaching objectives.

2. Connect with Your Audience

When you first walk out on stage, you have to be able to connect with the audience immediately. That doesn't mean you have to be *funny* immediately. First, you need to create space and be the focal point; in short, you need to have the audience's permission to be there.

You have about sixty seconds to make that connection—unless you are an A-lister. You can use many effective techniques, but self-deprecation often works best. By channeling all that energy against yourself before you go on stage and then actually taking a hit early, you release the audience's pent-up "make me laugh" energy. And you do it through laughter. What a powerful tool! It communicates that you are one of them.

Two business examples come to mind.

The CFO of a new client tore into me on the first day, telling me that all consultants were a waste of time, and that he hated paying me to tell him what he already knew. I asked him to give me a chance. He said he was so sure I would fail, he would walk around with a sandwich board singing my praises in public if I added value. Everyone knew about the bet. When he showed up with the sandwich board and wore it throughout the cafeteria for an hour, he won the hearts and minds of the team, while singing my praises. A win-win!

One of my mentors was a big idea visionary. He never failed do communicate in a humorous way that he had no talent for execution. As a result of his self-deprecation, his staff always had his back when it came to execution.

3. Use Callbacks

When things go well, the audience feels aligned and part of the experience, and laughter flows freely. Good comics and leaders build a story and take the group where they want to go. Sometimes an astute leader takes the group where *they* want to go.

A "callback," a reference to an earlier line or joke, creates identification and common ground. When I performed stand-up in Sweden, as an American outsider, I deliberately reacted to Swedish culture as part of my routine.

For example, throughout the show, I intentionally over-pronounced their word "*nej*" (which means "no") as one of my callbacks. It got laughs the first time because of the way I pronounced it. "I have one word for Swedish fermented fish: '*neeeeej*.'" That laid the foundation for using the callback later in the show.

Later in the routine, when the audience heard me say "I have one word for . . .," the audience chimed in with me and shouted out, "*Nej*!" They had anticipated the joke and punch line.

When a comic repeats a callback, the audience typically feels included on the inside joke. In business, "callbacks" create the same effect.

For example, in my former company, we often used "connecting the front line to the bottom line" as a callback and slogan.

Good leaders know that callbacks resonate in conversations and include them consistently in their daily messaging and conversations. They work as familiar reminders of the journey you share together and generate a sense of inclusion.

4. Probe, Accept Feedback, and Take Risks

As discussed earlier, probing, reflection, and feedback are critical for continuous growth. I always probed the audience and made sure I listened to their responses—whether crowd chatter before the show or comments during a routine. I had a reservoir of material, but I chose my lines based on the unique makeup of the collective personality gathered at the club each night.

In the course of a show, gaps and flat moments almost inevitably happen. But it's important not to dwell on them. Robin Williams was a master at this. Because of his rapid pace, he could move seamlessly to the next joke if a line didn't work.

Likewise, good leaders try new things. They float ideas with people they trust and willingly risk falling flat. Failing from time to time doesn't matter when you have the skill set and commitment to move on and not get paralyzed. If something doesn't work, try something else.

Pay attention to feedback because it allows you to adjust quickly when needed. I would write jokes, thinking the punch line would be X, when actually it turned out to be Y. I adjusted it in real time based on the audience response.

For example, I had written a joke for my time in Sweden about blaming the killing of the prime minister of Sweden on Lee Harvey Oswald. The first night I told it, I thought the laughter would come from blaming Lee Harvey Oswald. What was funnier was the path of the magic bullet, and the more outrageous I made it, the more they laughed. It wasn't the beginning and the end as I had thought.

I taped every show so I could play back what worked and what didn't, and I noted where I fell flat. You can't tape every meeting or conversation, but you can take notes (make sure you keep a notebook with you at all times). Jot it all down. Take note of what works in your staff meetings.

Active listening will help you find the right action sooner. Pay attention to the content as well as the emotion in your team's and employees' reactions. Don't get trapped in long sessions of analyzing *why* things failed. Instead, ask *what* you need to do next. Taking action toward an outcome always works better than too much focus on why you failed.

5. Manage Hecklers
(The Curious Case of the Drunk Duck)

At a club outside Stockholm, a drunk stared at me as I took the microphone. I had been watching him sitting up front with his buddies, who had all consumed copious amounts of alcohol well before the show started. As I opened my routine, he began to quack really loudly. At the end of every line I delivered, he said, "Quack, quack, quack." The audience laughed, and that emboldened him.

I had three options: work past him, challenge him, or defuse him. Those are the same options my clients have during any disruption: ignore, respond, or use the moment to create a different dynamic. I stopped and listen internally—and then I knew what I had to do.

"Ladies and gentleman, it is obvious that this guy is way funnier than I am, so I am going to join you in the audience and please give a warm welcome to Mr. Duck!" The audience applauded as he made his way up to the stage, and I joined his friends in the front row.

He got up, took the microphone, and pulled out his best material: "Quack, quack, quack." The boos couldn't have come any faster. As security escorted him off the stage, I turned the mic over to the headliner, a good friend, because even if I had been the funniest comic for the remaining ten minutes of my gig, the audience would remember only the drunk Daffy Duck.

Sometimes you have to give in and let it go to fight another day. It takes being in tune with your audience and choosing not to fight every battle. It works the same for any manager and leader. Every day, leaders face a range of options and need to make choices. You never have enough time to do everything you want, so why would you respond to everything with the same intensity, energy, and stress?

When something out of the ordinary happens, view it as an opportunity to redirect that energy into creating growth and acceleration. Working with energy this way echoes the wisdom of martial arts, such as aikido or judo. Understanding and redirecting energy works for decision-makers too.

In business, you have to deal with hecklers, as well: the market, your customers, your employees. They will challenge you with the unexpected, and you can give them ground, risk making it worse, or bring them into the fold.

For both comics and business leaders to succeed, they must have a strong presence. Achieving that requires elements of rogue leadership: going inward and then responding with purpose to whatever shows up.

In the condensed space of a stand-up routine, there is an opportunity for reflection, action, risk, innovation, and alignment. The immediacy forces the comic, like a leader, to use all those tools. There is no other path to success.

22

GETTING THERE BY LETTING GO

Engage people with what they expect; it is what they are able to discern and confirms their projections. It settles them into predictable patterns of response, occupying their minds while you wait for the extraordinary moment—that which they cannot anticipate.

—Sun Tzu, *The Art of War*

Every day, events unfold, results and risks emerge, and decisions have to be made. Believing we can stay on top of all that is an illusion.

Managers and leaders must plan ahead and develop strategies. Without good, well-thought-out plans and the actions to execute them, organizations stumble and eventually fall and fail. That goes without saying.

What is also true is that within any plan, there has to be some space for adjustments and corrections. When things go off the rails, many managers are stuck on executing what their plans, and can't move beyond what structure they had originally set out. In sports, would it make sense for a team who had a game plan to stick with the original plan if they were losing with two minutes to go?

You can't simply impose your plan on reality—you need to be flexible, open to change, and willing and able to make adjustments as you go from point A to point B. World-class teams spend a great deal of time up front talking through those contingencies and potential risks. They not only prepare for things to change: *they expect it.*

You will most likely sabotage your project if you adopt the attitude "We will move forward as we have planned, come hell or high water." Tempting fate like that almost guarantees that "hell or high water" will arrive one day.

A second, more sinister part of the illusion is our attempt to control *everything.* Pure and simple: *you can't.* When you recognize that you will have to improvise at times, and course correct, you actually have more of a chance of being successful.

Frequently, as an improvisation actor, my troupe would play improvisational theater games, such as First Line, Last Line. The audience would give a first line, such as "Mary, the garbage disposal is stuffed up with gunk," and the audience would suggest a completely unrelated last line, such as "My accountant needs us to review our charitable donations by Friday." The actors would have to start the scene with the first line and somehow arrive at that last line using logical, natural dialogue during the scene.

We succeeded every time. Why? Because within the structure there was room to change and respond to what was emerging in real time, while still keeping our eye on the goal of completing the scene successfully.

TELLING YOUR STORY

Reinventing Who You Are

I am what I am.

—Popeye

Many of the leaders I work with feel trapped by how others view them. Some have arrived at a new job with a reputation that preceded them. Still others were promoted, and now have to lead former colleagues and peers, changing the dynamics of established relationships.

How you show up defines you. The quickest way to change others' perceptions of you is by shaking things up and behaving in a different and more powerful manner. Words alone won't do the trick— you must follow through with purposeful actions that match your words.

ALABAMA SHAKES: CHANGING THE STATUS QUO

Jimmy Johns was promoted to Operations Director after being a part of the team for many years. He had a strong understanding of the business, the technical skill set, and engaging partnerships with customers.

Some of his colleagues viewed him as a good-ol' boy who took care of his network and based a lot of his decisions on long-term relationships. Rightly or wrongly, people at work believed that Jimmy played favorites.

When an Israeli firm purchased his company, the change forced him out of his comfortable bubble. He had to demonstrably break old habits to let people know the old Jimmy had moved on, especially in his new role. The change scared him, but he also knew he had to do it.

When we discussed his strategy for going forward, I emphasized the wisdom of shifting things slowly. We chose to tackle Jimmy's perceived favoritism as the first target. Any abrupt about-face would likely have backfired. I call this "micro change"—gradual and consistent change that moves forward, but not abrupt. Shaking things up, but at a slower pace.

Over time, Jimmy found he could shift his approach by adjusting his communication style, listening more actively, expanding his open-door policy that was previously selective on who he saw, and hold more powerful conversations on the shop floor. This approach might not work for everyone or in every situation—but it's a good option to add to your leadership tool kit. In doing so, he grew as a leader, and strengthened his ability to drive performance.

THE VISIBILITY TRAP

For years, leaders have tried "management by walking around." In the seminal *The One Minute Manager* (William Morrow, 2003), Ken Blanchard emphasizes that what you do as a manager carries more power than the amount of time you walk around.

Powerful leaders understand that *how* they show up makes the biggest impact.

But visibility can backfire, especially when it doesn't work as intended or when it isn't authentic.

How often have you heard the well-worn lines "I have an open-door policy" or "I'm on site every day"? Those words and habits mean nothing if the boss doesn't listen, cuts off communication, or dominates the conversation.

Here are other complaints I've heard from employees: "She only shows up for the barbecue but couldn't care less about us"; and "He's here just because the boss is in town." The workforce and middle managers know a dog and pony show when they see one.

SPECIAL VICTIMS UNIT

Many leaders lament that how they are seen is not fair—the work-force doesn't know them, and changing that is out of their control. But nothing is further from the truth.

You might think, *I'm not going to change who I am—my people should take the time to get to know me.* Why waste energy and time waiting when you can accelerate the effort by getting out there?

My client Brent was whining that he was recently placed in charge of a workforce that saw him as an asshole and didn't give him any credit. His frustration grew every day. I told him the solution was simple: Stop being an asshole. He rarely spent time with his team, never had a true open-door policy, and communicated by email whenever possible, versus making personal visits or phone calls.

Take some time to think about how you want to be seen, and what that looks like. Then start being that person. Pretty simple, but often ignored.

If you want to earn your workforce's trust and respect, be purposeful when you show it. Take charge. Authenticity, combined with accessibility, is powerfully effective.

CREATING PRESENCE AND VISIBILITY

My presence speaks volumes before I say a word.

—Mos Def, musician

Two fields of energy occur simultaneously in all of us. The one that we present to the world is mostly rehearsed, masked, and habitual. The inner field, often hidden from ourselves, influences our perception of reality.

—Kati Pressman, author, *Simple Presence*

People underrate presence. It has to do with not only the way we show up, but also the "echo" or after effect that stays behind when we leave. Think of how a room feels when someone has left—you can still feel their presence, even in their physical absence.

Presence acts as a driver and guide, a motivator and influencer—all day, every day. This applies in the world of business as much as it does elsewhere in our lives. Effective leaders do not have to be physically present every moment to have an impact and fill the "visceral space" within their organizations.

So, we can categorize presence in two ways:

1. Present presence: how people perceive you as you physically interact with them

2. Absent presence: how you influence people when you're no longer physically present

PRESENT PRESENCE

You can physically be in a room talking to someone, but not be *mentally* present. We have all had similar moments with our loved ones. Just ask my first wife.

As the cliché says, "Showing up is half the battle." But it's not enough to just show up. When mentally and physically *present*, you listen better. You hear more. You notice things you might otherwise miss. Being fully present gives you access to more information.

That's why active listening tops the list of important skills for any leader. Be an observer first, before acting as a player in the scene. The time for action comes later.

Top tips for being truly present:

1. Seek to understand.

2. Confirm and reconfirm what you think you heard.

3. Ask lots of questions—and make sure most of them are open-ended. Open ended questions and careful listening are a part of being present with someone.

4. Have a conversation, not an interview.

5. Surprise people in their workplace and ask for a few minutes of their time.

6. Ask people what worries or concerns them and get their input on decisions you have to make.

7. Participate in informal non-agenda "hall chats," which often bear the greatest fruit.

8. Make eye contact.

9. Always express thanks at the end of a dialogue, whether in formal meetings or an informal chat.

ABSENT PRESENCE

The impact of your absence depends on what you do when you're physically present: *Present presence shapes absent presence.* By making sure you always remain mentally alert and responsive to your team when you interact with them, you will greatly improve your impact when you need to tend to business elsewhere. Your vision, ideas, and attributes can continue to drive your team to execute your plans and strategies.

Creating a transformative work environment depends on the quality and effectiveness of a leader's "absent presence."

Absent presence helps long-term stability and sustainability because your team no longer relies on your physical presence in order to feel inspired by your leadership. They become less dependent on you. Some organizations still feel the impact and influence of great leaders even years after they have left.

Liz Chandler, a coach on my team, had a profound impact on her client group. They came to rely on her support and ability to help them move forward. When she left the project, the team knew they had to carry on without her. They made up wristbands that said, "WWLD" ("What would Liz do?). She left that project a long time ago, yet they still wear those wristbands to this day. How many of us leave that kind of legacy?

Part of that legacy is always built on understanding and trust. If a leader is accessible, shows genuine interest in how to support his or her team, and acts upon that information in a positive way, the legacy can be strengthened.

25

GENERATING INFLUENCE

The key to successful leadership today is influence, not authority.

—Ken Blanchard, author

Showing up really matters, as we saw in the previous chapter. Understanding how you show up matters even more. Many leaders fail to notice how their employees, clients, and stakeholders see them.

Rogue leaders ask themselves, "What happens to my organization as I move through it?" When you can observe the impact you have, you can make a big difference in leadership effectiveness. Consider it a part of emotional intelligence.

Many books and articles explain how to cultivate this kind of self-awareness—suffice it to say that it all hinges on being detached and honest enough to watch yourself in action.

Let's use a biological analogy: The body undergoes chemical and electrical changes in response to external force fields. Your mere presence will affect the space you are observing. Every action you take changes the relationship between you and the external "force field" that always surrounds you.

Over time, it is possible to create a critical mass of influential employees who will change your organization's thinking and behavior. Malcolm Gladwell's book *The Tipping Point* (Little, Brown, 2000) explains how this happens. You don't need everyone on board, just the influencers at every level of your organization.

So how do I know who the influencers are at all levels of my organization? And how do I interact effectively with them?

Power lies in ongoing adjustments. Doing this effectively involves "taking the temperature" of your environment and making course corrections in real time—on the job, not at an event or in some other space external to daily business management.

You want your team to ask questions and/or express concerns or insights every day. When feedback happens constantly, you don't need to schedule full-on feedback mechanisms like surveys, upward feedback, and 360-degree circles.

I don't suggest you become a hyped-up feedback machine (that might be too "out-there" for your leadership style). You can attend to feedback quietly. I remember one executive who demanded feedback after every interaction with his team—it felt exhausting at times and therefore lost its impact.

The point: You should seek and receive information constantly in a way comfortable for you. Engage in active listening. The quality of your awareness and emotional intelligence actively affect your team's growth and development. You will likely find that many little daily steps turn out to be more powerful in changing the culture and performance than any grand initiative.

Here are three methods to get that much-needed input.

1. Stone-Skipping

It makes sense to be purposeful about what you do—or at least be aware of the effect you have on others. Intuitive leaders understand that the energy from their actions continues spreading, even when they no longer notice the effects. This is similar to the ripple effect from throwing a stone in the middle of a pond.

To use stone-skipping in your organization, pick small, unobtrusive, and benign ways to continually test the waters with new ideas. Challenge your team. Like a skipping a stone, you continually create feedback that guides your movement. Pay attention and notice if you encounter any resistance. If so, it might be time to float new ideas (pun intended) and see where it takes you.

2. Pulsing

In a similar, but slightly different way, "pulsing" involves asking for feedback instead of trying something and passively observing reactions and feedback. Like sending out a probe, pulsing directs movement and responses, and when done right it can be non-disruptive and discreet. Open-ended questions work best.

I sometimes hear people ask, "Do you want the truth or do you want 'the right answer'?" I have heard this time and again, but put like that, the question leaves no real way for the person responding to be candid, because you have given them a binary choice.

Similarly, questions such as "That was a great meeting, wasn't it?" "People loved my speech, did you?" aren't designed for feedback, but confirmation. In a legal context, this qualifies as "leading the witness." Frontloading questions this way will not generate real feedback.

Try these "pulsing" questions on your team:

1. How did that go over?
2. What was my message?
3. What did you hear I was concerned about?
4. What was your takeaway from the meeting?
5. What is your understanding?
6. How could I have improved that?
7. What fell flat, if anything?
8. What were your top three takeaways?
9. What would you do differently?
10. Have I missed an important point?

3. Another Source of Feedback: Coaches

Having served as a coach, I do not need to sing the praises of coaching here (it could be perceived as a conflict of interest). Nevertheless, why do we value coaching in sports, yet tend to suspect its efficacy in business?

Many leaders who resist coaching do so because of a perceived stigma attached to having a coach, which incorrectly assumes that the client must be deficient in some way and doesn't know it all. In reality, of course, no one knows it all (even Einstein would have benefited from coaching in mathematics!). Very few understand that a good coach can help accelerate performance—not merely by correcting errors but also, if not more, by building on skills and strengths. This works as much in the business world as in sports.

Some people fear that by using a coach, their achievements won't be fully credited, or that somehow, they needed help because their leadership skills lacked something crucial.

If you have the opportunity to use a coach—a thinking partner— grab it immediately. View it as a rare opportunity.

You might say, "I can't afford to hire a coach." In that case, find a mentor or someone outside the organization willing to give you candid, tough feedback. If you think you know it all, you have much to learn.

Whatever you choose, at the end of the day, find a good feedback source. Again, I firmly believe getting a good coach works best, but you can generate feedback many other ways if you truly can't invest in a coach.

It's now time to look at the fuel for creating presence and influence: clear communication.

RECAP
Part 5: Showing Up with Purpose

1. Connect with your people authentically.

2. Observe and get feedback continually.

3. Be flexible as the environment changes.

4. Know your story and tell it well.

5. Be willing to probe, take risks, and adjust if necessary.

6. Ask open-ended questions.

7. Create common ground.

PART 6

COMMUNICATING WITH SIMPLICITY

To successfully communicate a message of any complexity in this digital age you must understand that audiences are swimming in excessive data. You must be kind to them and throw them a life preserver.

—Frank Pietrucha, author,
Supercommunicator: Explaining the
Complicated So Anyone Can Understand

THE ART OF COMMUNICATION

The art of communication is the language of leadership.

—James Humes, author

The single biggest problem with communication is the illusion that it has taken place.

—George Bernard Shaw, playwright

My client looked at me and said, "I sent them an email. Why didn't they do what I asked them?" Yep: a bad case of *"they are the problem."*

Blaming others for our own inadequacies happens a lot, especially in the business world. For example, if you send an email expecting some action in response, simply "checking the box" that you sent the email won't get the results you want—unless you specifically make a request. You must take responsibility for not only checking items off your to-do list, but also making sure you *communicate clearly.*

Being clear brings powerful meaning to your message. Would you be inspired by something like this: "We need to ask ourselves how we can contribute to our country and society, instead of waiting around for the government to help and assist us"? Zzzzz.

JFK had a much different delivery: "Ask not what your country can do for you—ask what you can do for your country." Direct and effective.

It might seem like a paradox, but simple communication allows us to express complex ideas more easily. It also is effective for motivating others as well as sharpening our focus and objectives, so people know what we want to achieve. In short, words do matter a great deal.

You have probably seen the iconic graphic for communication depicting a sender and receiver with a signal channel or line connecting them. The image usually also shows some "noise" on the line that blocks clear transmission of the signal. A communication breakdown!

Obviously, this applies to all sorts of communications—from phones to radio transmissions—as well as direct mouth-to-ear communication. It's not enough to speak and be heard—we also need to speak with clarity and intent to avoid any unintended "noise" that distorts what we have to say.

Even though talking face-to-face isn't perfect, it helps us avoid the many pitfalls that occur with other modes of communication. Memos, statements, and so on can work—especially when dealing with officials such as lawyers or accountants or keeping the stakeholders happy—but nothing works like face-to-face. Period.

Social media channels can be useful for sending out a consistent message, but they can't replace the in-person, interactive conversations. Unfortunately, posts, tweets, and other forms of social media exchanges are passive, so we often don't know how our communication landed.

We need to keep in mind the difference between "active" and "passive" communication, and the difference between simplicity and unnecessary complexity.

My mom had become part of an improvisational theater group that supported a mime (who shall remain nameless). He said his grandmother told him that he had only a limited amount of words in life, and that once he used them up he would have no more—and so he became a mime. Aside from the fact that he was full of BS, I liked the story. It was a reminder that we should always chose our messages with care and take the time to do so.

To communicate effectively, you first need to establish a connection. Most of us don't take the time to do it or to do it well. Too often, we broadcast whatever comes to mind and then don't even check to make sure the signal gets through.

The following lists show the different ways our communications can be received by others (it depends on the quality of our delivery) if we focus only on our message:

Positives:

✎ They understood what you said/communicated (*objective achieved*).

Negatives

✎ They might not understand.

✎ They might not pay attention.

- They interpreted the message differently.

- They took offense to a word you used.

- They didn't like it.

- They went home and ranted on Facebook.

- They trolled you later.

- They talked about you at their next therapy session.

Note: There is one positive outcome and a lot of negative potential outcomes. And yet we continue to talk/blog/post/email without paying attention to how we are being received.

In Frank Pietrucha's stellar book *Supercommunicator: Explaining the Complicated So Anyone Can Understand* (AMACOM, 2014) he describes some guidelines worth repeating here:

Guidelines for Effective Communication

1. Put your main idea up front.

2. Write short sentences and short paragraphs.

3. Use active voice.

4. Use conventional words.

5. Be correct, credible, and complete.

6. Keep it brief.

Tips for effective verbal communication follow a similar pattern.

Most of all, as covered earlier in chapter 21, "Stand-Up Leadership," regardless of the type of communication, you need to understand your audience. Choose words that resonate with them.

THE TARZAN PRINCIPLE FOR SIMPLE COMMUNICATION

"Me No Like Big Words"

Is an intelligent human being likely to be much more than a large-scale manufacturer of misunderstanding?

—Philip Roth, author

Simple communication, unburdened by excess words and jargon, is much more powerful. Yet we often ignore that truth. Here are seven compelling reasons why we do so at our peril.

1. Focus on clarity. Like oil in an engine, clarity "lubricates" communication. Know what you want in clear simple terms and communicate as such. Remember, "less is more." The likelihood that your message will get misconstrued increases the more you add to it—as happens when it goes through layers of staff. "I hear she asked us all for alignment" can become "I hear she wants to institute solitary confinement." Monty Python captured the humor of the "telephone effect" in *Life of Brian*: "Blessed are the cheese makers and makers of all dairy products"—which started out as "Blessed are the peacemakers."

2. Avoid trophy words. A colleague of mine once used the term "asymptotic" during a meeting. I found a way to get it inserted into his annual review, and it passed our leadership without question. I am positive no one knew what it meant, but no one was going to admit they didn't know. But *I* asked.

3. Control your messaging. Like it or not, in the world of social media—for example, tweeting and texting—you have to keep it short and crisp. You control messaging by being concise. Think of it as "short is the new black." But you still must choose your words carefully—especially when using fewer of them. Make every word count.

4. Simplify. How's this for simplicity? "Evaluate the current environment with regards to the plethora of inputs that are being processed by your neuro-sensors, and thusly creating thoughts, which are generated in milliseconds transposed across your referent learning system to generate a response through the activation of words or activity as expressed by psycho-motor functionality, based on correct environmental conditions linked to your desired outcome." Hard to follow and understand, eh? Much more effective to simply say, "Pay attention before speaking."

5. Go one-on-one. Personalize as much as you can. Go speak to the person. They won't bite—usually.

6. Be authentic. Don't hide behind clichéd phrases—they tend to depersonalize communication. Take, for example, the phrase "emotional capital." Instead of telling your staff "The balance of our emotional capital has trended downward slightly this quarter," you could say, "We've had a challenging quarter." Some examples of other overused words: "key," "alignment," "integration," "robust," "outcomes." More often than not, these can ring hollow when they obscure what you really want to say—whether intentional or not.

7. **Stay consistent.** Repeat the same (or similar) words when expressing the same message. Repetition helps people remember important words. Used wisely, they can act like a mantra that burrows into the unconscious. The advertising industry has honed this skill to perfection.

SIMPLIFY EXTERNALS

You Can Handle the Truth

*My whole premise has been, right from the beginning,
that it would take me a lifetime to learn to explain
myself as an artist. As you grow older, you learn what
to do and what to leave out. You kind of simplify your
work and get the same thing done with fewer strokes.
It's pretty interesting to me.*

—Tony Bennett, singer

Not only does simplifying your communication get your point across more easily, but it helps simplify your life-simplifying is the only way to survive the barrage of stimuli and be effective.

Don't fall into the trap of pretending you can handle it all. You can't.

We all want to be heroes and show how well we can multitask; many leaders complicate their lives so much they become ineffective at everything.

As a business leader, you need to constantly ask, "What levers will drive my business forward?" To simplify, decide on three important issues instead of trying to make progress on twenty. Learning to prioritize takes practice and work, but once you master it, you will find yourself able to accomplish more with less effort.

I'm not just talking about time management; I'm talking about what you choose to engage with. When so much that crosses your desk seems amazing, fascinating, and fabulous, you soon discover that hardly any of it lives up to its promise. As we explored earlier in the book, taking a step back by going inward is critical.

Your initial response creates the next trigger and another response, and quickly you can find yourself overwhelmed trying to process everything that comes at you. The result: You deprive your team of growth and opportunities as you try to handle it all. When leaders constantly react to overwhelm, they stifle their organization's ability to be effective.

So how do you simplify?

1. Reduce the number of meetings, memos, and emails.

2. Opt for one-on-one meetings as often as possible.

3. Pick three key messages to communicate—never twenty.

4. Every week, pick four things that will make it a great week and then execute them.

5. Question everything you have committed to in your schedule and get clear on what value you get out of it. Do you schedule unnecessary meetings just because it's expected? Do you make sure the right people get the information they need to make decisions? Do any actions come out of it?

6. Use direct and clear language, especially in emails.

7. Limit yourself to a predetermined number of words in memos and emails to staff. Think Twitter, and try to match their limits. Yes, this might be tough, but it's great practice.

8. Ask your staff to write executive summaries on all documents and to attach details for backup.

9. Demand simplicity from those around you—especially in how they report to you, message you, or file reports.

How you communicate is important; what you communicate is critical. The message received by your team cannot be overemphasized.

RECAP
Part 6: Communicating with Simplicity

1. Keep your communication direct and simple; the fewer words the better.

2. Personal communication has greater impact than any memo or email.

3. Confirm that your message has been received and there are no misunderstandings.

4. Create alignment through key words or phrases, like a mantra.

5. Ask those around you to be concise and brief in their reporting and verbal communication with you; set the expectation.

6. Be consistent with your message—remember the one thing?

7. Say you understand only if you really do.

PART 7

LEADING FROM THE HEART

Leadership is all about emotional intelligence. Management is taught, while leadership is experienced.

—Rajeev Suri, CEO

THE POWER OF
THE PLAYGROUND

Unleashing Innovation and Collaboration

Play is the only way the highest intelligence of human-kind can unfold.

—Joseph Chilton Pearce, author

While playing golf today, I hit two good balls. I stepped on a rake.

—Henny Youngman, comic

Business is supposedly serious business. And so is life—if we make it that way. All young mammals instinctively love to play. Just think of little puppies or kittens, not to mention human children. Play helps train and shape the brain for the more serious business of living later on as adults. Play teaches us roles, communication, creativity, innovation, and, ultimately, pure joy.

Play releases stress and creates common bonds and collaboration. No matter our background, socioeconomic status, or the car we drive, play deepens relationships and strips away formalities that stifle creativity and spontaneity.

Play takes many forms. I remember my mother working at a psychiatric hospital as the head nurse. One day, she and other members of the staff sat with patients in the yard and participated in their painting session. A government VIP who came to discuss the work of the hospital joined the group, never having met my mom.

Thinking she was a patient, he went over to her and, in a patronizing tone, asked her name.

"Kati," she replied.

"And what are we doing today, Kati?"

"Painting," she said.

"Do you like painting?"

She nodded. "I love painting."

"You're good at it too."

My mom asked, "Can I hug you?"

"Of course," he said, and she gave him a warm hug.

He had assumed she was a patient and treated her accordingly.

She ignored the VIP's patronizing formality by continuing her playful attitude. When he realized who she was later in her office, it changed the dynamic of their conversation. In the meeting, the government official dropped his formal tone when addressing my mother. Her playfulness had softened his armor, and he opened up more.

Comics on stage use improvisation as a form of playing with the audience. Some of the best comedy groups—such as the Groundlings, Second City, and Saturday Night Live—have used improvisation to create memorable sketches. Then why not use it in business to create something of value?

The power of improvisation comes from giving each other permission to play and fail. Yes, you must follow rules within a defined structure, but this guides you to be creative while doing what's best for the team. It must be handled skillfully—and that takes practice.

Trainers and leaders in the business world often use improvisation to improve synergy and team building. Invariably, participants get a much richer experience than from a typical offsite brainstorming session with flip charts.

The more open a structure, the more creative the results. Too many retreats have such a narrow, rigid agenda that they impede creativity, almost guaranteeing limited results before the day has even begun. How often does an offsite meeting actually lead to significant change?

Of course, simply getting together away from the office routine can have its own benefits. Experiencing memorable moments together gives your team shared references they can draw on when they return to their desks in the "real" world.

When I meet former colleagues from a company I worked with for twenty-three years, we don't reminisce about the results. We talk about the time we spent together laughing or playing. No one says, "Remember our record year in last year?" or "How about that market strategy from five years ago?"

Examples of shared memories from my own business life include a soccer game in San Francisco's Golden Gate Park, where, as a goalie, I got kicked in the *cajones;* or the time we got snowed in at a resort and made snow angels.

Much research documents the role of play in development, yet as adults, we tend to avoid play whenever we engage in business—reserving it for weekends.

Whenever I ask leaders about who has influenced them and whom they trust, they often mention people they can laugh and play with. Having some fun together day to day typically ranks high on their list.

In her article *"Five Reasons You Need to Play More,"* reprinted in part here, with her permission, my colleague Emma Seppälä writes:

> Research finds that fun seriously aids everything you want your mind to do. Submerged in the responsibilities of life, the seriousness of world affairs, and an ever-growing to-do list, we often forget to *play*. Animals, on the other hand, continue to play throughout their adult lives! We may believe that play is somehow no longer appropriate or cast aside as a frivolous waste of time. Research suggests, however, that play is essential to our well-being, creativity, and health:

1. It boosts our creativity.

2. It helps us think outside the box.

3. It improves our health.

4. It makes us present.

5. It connects us.

As I described previously, social connectedness is a fundamental need for human beings. During World War I, on January 1, 1915, a soldier in the front line sent home a famous letter that was first published in the London *Times*. It described the events of the Christmas Day truce: "The English brought a soccer ball from the trenches, and pretty soon a lively game ensued. How marvelously wonderful, yet how strange it was. The German officers felt the same way about it. Thus Christmas, the celebration of love, managed to bring mortal enemies together as friends for a time.

This striking story is a reminder that play—the ability to laugh and let go, to inhabit the present, and to be immersed in the mirth and lightness of being—can be an ultimate act of love and belongingness. It reminds us of play as an all-important element in leadership, one that create collaboration and a sense of belonging to something greater than oneself.

Emma reinforces with clarity that there is power and value in play in the workplace.

CREATING A
SHARED STORY

We are all storytellers. We all live in a network of stories. There isn't a stronger connection between people than storytelling.

—Jimmy Neil Smith, storyteller

In modern society, we often think money motivates the workforce. On the contrary, research shows that most workers feel more motivated by other, more meaningful rewards—such as feeling their labor makes a difference. If you create a shared vision, your employees will feel connected to a greater good and go the extra mile for you, willingly increasing productivity. "Who are we?" If that question can be answered at all levels, you've done your job.

This effort requires more than circulating the mission statement and hanging nice motivating posters on the walls. Although knowing the organization's mission is important, most employees don't think about it in their day-to-day work—unless they happen to work for a very special company.

If employees don't hold the company vision in their hearts, even the best mission and vision statements will be ignored. They will look good only as PR on your social media feeds. Using corporate speak to communicate with employees alienates and demotivates them and often results in poor productivity.

Typically, leaders roll out their vision and ask their team to buy into it. But it is much more effective if you empower your team to participate in creating the organizational mission. After all, your company relies on them to implement it.

Warning: It takes more than going through the motions of getting input from everyone, filling up flip charts, and toasting work well done.

Rogue leaders take a different perspective: They make sure the team feels *connected* to both the mission and the leadership—and that means reinforcing the leadership-team connection every day.

Leaders achieve this by building a story—where employees identify as key characters in the organization's narrative. Good leaders also recognize and reward actions that align with the mission and add momentum to the narrative.

My first senior boss knew that instinctively. He quickly achieved quality connections with his team, and often across thousands of miles, without needing to frequently meet them face-to-face. He made it a priority to communicate with each of us regularly to ensure that we knew he supported us.

Others were not so successful. I remember a labor negotiation with my Swedish employees. It went well from my perspective, but the UK boss who managed me protested that he didn't like all the details Swedish laws require. He could see and appreciate things only from his bubble in the UK, even though the company was Swedish. He and I clashed constantly, but one thing finally got me in his corner: record-breaking results.

We didn't accomplish that by cutting costs or by insisting on unrealistic boosts in productivity. My team and I were successful by creating a shared story, one that still lives today among us whenever we touch base.

WRITE THE STORY—DON'T LET OTHERS DO IT FOR YOU

When I first met Ken McKenzie, managing director of Premdor, a large door manufacturing plant in the UK, he already knew what he wanted his company's story to be. He wanted to be the dominant player in the market and go from 20 percent market share to a majority share. We talked about his company's culture and why he would play an important part in achieving his goals.

His workforce came from the surrounding coal mining area, so he had to deal with many long-standing labor issues and clashes with management. Major strikes and even violence had rocked that region. Ken wanted his workers to take pride in what they did and how they did it. Previous leaders had allowed the team to set the story as "we are the best of a bad bunch," with a hard line between management and the workforce.

Ken did things differently, focusing on five things: engaging effectively with the front line; creating business acumen for all team members; involving the entire supply chain; challenging old norms; and recognizing the workforce.

The story he crafted focused on overtaking the competition, not by being the best of the worst, but by being *the best of the best.*

All the parties involved had to earn one another's trust, and this meant a major shift in how management and employees related to each other. At first, senior leaders stuck to their old ways, and frontline supervisors identified heavily as victims along with their people.

Over time, Ken included more of the workforce in conversations and discussions, and he showed up consistently for them. Word traveled fast that the managing director sat down and openly communicated with and *listened to* a supervisor—in front of management and invited guests. This meeting between front line and the MD had such a powerful impact, it paved the way for fuller engagement with the entire team.

By openly interacting with his team and treating them with respect, Ken reinforced the story he wanted for his company. He didn't need to keep repeating it. Implicitly, he embodied it in everything he did. He demonstrated that he cared about his employees and wanted them involved in managing the business.

TOUCHSTONING

Ken knew how to tell a story: build it live every day in the workplace—then reinforce it in every hallway meeting. I call this approach "touchstoning." It provides a common and familiar reference for people. They feel included.

Remember our discussion about comedy and how we can use it as a tool—for example, using the callback technique (see "Use Callbacks" in chapter 21). Inside jokes link the comic with the audience.

For a corporate story to work, it needs an underlying core message that connects every other message about the organization's direction and identifies key priorities, especially your organization's *raison d'être*—your purpose, your *why*.

While on the shop floor, Ken would naturally refer to moments when the team or an employee stepped up or remind the team of where they were a year ago and how far they had come.

Touchstoning keeps the common references alive and circulating in the lifeblood of the company. It creates daily opportunities to remind everyone why they come to work. Once you have the touchstoning references circulating, the messaging moves faster each time.

MIND THE GAP

Effective leaders know the power of "controlling the message." This means making sure words and actions consistently match to create alignment. Without sufficient information, people instinctively fill in the blanks—usually with a negative spin. Far too many organizations leave these "message gaps" wide open, and as a result, the core message gets distorted and frustration and a lack of motivation become the norm.

Demotivation can come about in a number of ways: the frontline worker who offers a great idea to improve the company yet never hears back, the executive left out of the loop on a new project, the unilateral decisions made by the top brass without input from the rank and file.

Such motivational devastation can be easily avoided by making sure that everyone feels they matter to the organization and that the corporate story remains front and center at all times.

THE HALL OF SHAME

To create and maintain a motivating, all-inclusive story for your company, you would do well to remove the following words and phrases from your lexicon:

"You'll know when we know."

"Not your pay grade."

"We are working on it."

"I didn't think you needed to know."

"I sent you an email—you mean you didn't you get it?"

"I've been busy."

"I didn't think you'd be interested."

"Great idea!" (then take credit for it later.)

"My dog ate it." (Well, okay, not that one.)

Comments like these (often unintentional) make it harder to lead. They disconnect and alienate people. Be more mindful of the words you use, avoid clichés and put-downs; instead, develop the habit of using conversations with your team to reinforce the company's most powerful messages. Be and act as your organization's lead "storyteller." You'll be amazed by the difference.

$$\left(\begin{array}{c} 31 \end{array}\right)$$

CULTIVATING
PARTNER LEADERSHIP

True leaders understand that leadership is not about them, but about those they serve. It is not about exalting themselves, but about lifting others up.

—Sheri L. Dew, author and CEO

Scoreboards, KPIs, and graphs all make performance visible and should form a part of any leader's tool kit. Keeping track of progress and measuring scores (how well you meet your goals), while often overlooked, remain critical to any business.

When you and your team understand the results, whether good or bad, you're in a better position to make adjustments. Quantitative feedback helps keep everything on target. If you don't know your progress score, you can't play the game well.

This information also helps unify everyone, whatever their role, and helps avoid the "us and them" mentality seen in many companies. Your company's well-being should be the overarching driver for all action, across all departments. Fragmented decision-making often spells disaster for organizations.

Values-based leadership creates the ideal work environment and thus leads to top performance. Employees as well as shareholders benefit. These values can be expressed in many ways in the workplace—for example, rewarding work mutual respect, opportunities to grow and develop, and benefits to the community.

Providing benefits for all stakeholders often produces other unforeseen benefits—as Ken McKenzie's UK story shows: He wanted his customers, shareholders, and employees to share the benefits of tangible bottom-line results.

He aimed to instill values such as an empowered workforce, customer service, "right first time" quality, pride in work, and employee advancement. He wanted his suppliers and clients to be excited about the fact they worked with *his* company. He wanted the market to view his company, services, and products as providing great value.

Premdor offers lessons for everyone. Their management made sure the daily work felt like a partnership rather than the usual transactional arrangement: "I'll give you eight hours, and you'll give me a paycheck." Everyone experienced something more meaningful.

Workers were given the space and coaching support to manage their own business area, such as the door press or the joining workshop. Premdor invited suppliers and clients to work on solutions and risk management together.

These previously excluded members helped create value for everyone in the supply chain. To support the overall health of the business, they agreed to do things they hadn't done before. The entire supply chain tackled previous taboos, such as discussing profit margins and opening up the financial books without giving away trade secrets. Such common-ground management opened doors (pun intended) for the benefit of all.

Ken changed the way he did business when he said, "If you want to be a supplier, employee, or a client, this is how we will work. And if you work this way, you will benefit because everyone's business will increase."

SUSTAINABILITY

Keeping the Mojo Going

Sustainability is a part of our 'rise' philosophy. You cannot rise if you take more from the community than you put back.

—Anand Mahindra, entrepreneur

"Money" isn't a bad word. Profits are good. That's what companies are created for: to generate profits. I believe that if you lead with heart, you will make more profits, increase sustainability, and benefit both your employees and community in innumerable ways.

A single company might achieve total market domination yet have little in terms of sustainable value. Companies that achieve both tend to improve profits as well as community relations. A commitment to sustainability and to minimizing any disruptive long-term impact on the local community generates goodwill and promotes innovation and growth.

"Value" means more than the financial bottom line—if you aim for value in everything you do, the bottom line will take care of itself. *How* you generate profits makes a big difference. Good leaders not only take care of profits, but also cultivate synergy to unite their teams and align values. I have worked with executives and leaders who have increased my sustainable awareness, and I always aim to pay it forward by sharing what I've learned about sustainable practices.

Recent studies and analyses show that brands that display sustainability values—for example, in packaging and marketing materials—increase sales.

"Consumers around the world are saying loud and clear that a brand's social purpose is among the factors that influence purchase decisions," according to Amy Fenton, global leader of public development and sustainability. "This behavior is on the rise, and it provides opportunities for meaningful impact in our communities, in addition to helping to grow share for brands."

More than ever, we are asked to focus on our eco-footprint and our social responsibility in the marketplace. Values-based companies, such as Atlassian, that give back to the community inspire other like-minded enterprises to monitor their social and environmental impact.

You *can* be profitable and have a heart. Many CEOs believe you can run a thriving business based on value principles, where profitability must fit into a broader set of values. Businesses now commonly speak of "ecosystems"—often to refer to their own suite of services or products, as well as to how these fit into a wider network of influences. Less socially responsible companies adopt a more shortsighted view and focus on quick returns that boost their bottom line and only take care of shareholders.

In Costa Rica, the government pays for women in bordering Nicaragua to come to their country for prenatal care. Clearly, an act of altruism, but also a form of self-protection: A local community member explained to me, "If our neighbors are healthy, we are too." They understand that if things are okay in the "local" neighborhood, the larger society will benefit as well.

Heart-based leadership does work—and works well—but the values must come from the top and be crystalized in action throughout the organization. Otherwise, we are left with yet another fancy mission and vision statement, but little else. People know if you really care, or if your big-check donations only serve to give you a PR photo op. As a leader, you can do both: serve and support your community *and* make a good profit.

Sustainability brings to mind the environment. Population growth, climate change, and access to education and essentials such as clean water will challenge everyone on the planet. This already affects your present and future clients.

More and more consumers are making choices based not on what product or services to buy, but on who sells them. Concern for societal and planetary well-being goes beyond charitable donations or 10K-run sponsorships.

Decide who you want to be, and then work with your shareholders about cultivating a collective "heart." You have to know and follow your own moral compass and observe the impact you have on the community and your employees. That focus should rightfully permeate your work, just as much as, if not more than, monitoring profit and loss.

Sandja Brügmann of the Passion Institute calls it "conscious leadership." I can't think of a better term for it, as it combines the heart, the mind, and the pocketbook. And where does conscious leadership have the most impact? On your people.

RECAP
Part 7: Leading from the Heart

1. Use play to stimulate creativity, release stress, and build collaboration.

2. Develop a shared story to align your team.

3. Refer to your shared story often to stay on the chosen path.

4. Avoid demotivating responses that create anger and frustration.

5. Achieve success in your business and community by adopting a sustainability mindset.

6. Improve your bottom line by partnering with stakeholders. You are all on the same team, playing in the same game.

PART 8

ENGAGING THE FRONT LINE

An exceptional company is the one that gets all the little details right. And the people out on the front line, they know when things are not going right, and they know when things need to be improved. And if you listen to them, you can soon improve all those niggly things which turns an average company into an exceptional company.

—Richard Branson, entrepreneur

EN GARDE

Winning the Battle and the War

To be nobody-but-yourself—in a world which is doing its best, night and day, to make you everyone else— means to fight the hardest battle which any human being can fight; and never stop fighting.

—E. E. Cummings, author

Now that we have all our tools ready to go, let's take a look at a good battle plan—one that leads to long-term performance, a motivated team, success, and a positive impact on both your workforce and the community at large. You don't have to sacrifice one or the other.

SHORT-CIRCUITING THE ORG CHART

If "business as usual" is failing to help you reach your business objectives, you can break the stranglehold by turning off a single circuit breaker. You don't need to go overboard and shut down the whole grid.

You need only enroll an "influential power field" (employee or team member) and do something very simple: talk face-to-face. You could bring in two or three others—the number doesn't matter. Just having a simple, interpersonal conversation can blow up an energy field and release pent-up creativity and productivity. In this role, you become the disruptor.

Our power comes not from gigabytes of data but from our shared humanity. At the end of the day, decisions must be made by *us*, not by data or apps or graphs. I can't think of a more powerful tool than getting out of the office and actually speaking with someone.

Shakespeare has always been a source of wisdom for me—the story of *Henry V* in particular. (You may not have heard of him, because he has zero followers on Instagram and Twitter).

At Agincourt, France, the English king's troops are preparing for battle the next morning. His troops are outnumbered by the French at least five to one. They have given up hope, expecting nothing short of a slaughter.

Henry has two options: choose a self-fulfilling prophesy or attempt to do something different.

That night, the king goes out disguised as a soldier and walks among his troops. He finds them demoralized, thinking they are all doomed.

Come morning, he rallies the troops and boosts morale with a rousing appeal to heroism and the greatness of England. Together, they hatch a cunning plan, and against the odds, Henry's troops succeed in routing the French that day. Both in the play and in history. No app, no data, and no tool could have done that. Instead, Henry created a vision, a sense of something greater in his troops.

PLAN THE PLAN

The English also won the battle because the king asked his troops to come up with a plan based on the reality they saw. Most plans fail because organizations spend less time on the planning and more time on executing. This harkens back to the need to take action we discussed earlier in the book. Any action is going to be more robust if everyone involved is part of the process and there is space to get ready for its execution. Anything worth doing should be given the time and focus well before you do it.

My oil client had an issue with the decay of pipeline and the risk of incidents and emissions. He brought all stakeholders together, even contractors, and, they went step-by-step through the entire plan for the inspection process. Anyone who touched the project had a voice.

These often-excluded voices (such as contractors) brought their ideas and expertise to the table, and assumptions made about every step were challenged and vetted. The result? A significant reduction in cost and risk—as well as the discovery of a potential alternative testing method that would save the company millions.

(34)

BECOME THE BANDLEADER
The Magic of Rhythm

Life is about rhythm. We vibrate, our hearts are pumping blood, we area a rhythm machine, that's what we are.

—Mickey Hart, musician

The good life is a process, not a state of being. It is a direction not a destination.

—Carl Rogers, author

Our days ebb and flow. When things get out of whack with our daily rhythm, we begin to affect others around us. Organizations or departments within an organization need to balance inputs and outputs to maintain optimum health.

When leaders run their organization with a consistent approach, it adds order and serenity to the workplace. It also provides a continuum of relationship as well as space from which to make decisions, take action, learn lessons, and respond to the outside world's challenges.

While having a defined structure and schedule, you also need to allow for flexibility, which might seem counterintuitive. Above all, be sure to avoid rigidity to the point of paralysis.

Your structure needs to allow new ideas and processes to enter the system and remain open enough to respond to unexpected inputs. Growth occurs only when an organization "metabolizes" incoming energy and information. Certain interactions, transactions, and exchanges must take place every day for your organization to thrive and remain healthy. It has to have the right "beat."

If you execute decisions and communicate and operate in a consistent manner, you will remain on the right path.

Some call this "the battle," while others call it "cadence"—the familiar hum of the daily cycle as your people take care of business. Success does not depend on a series of meetings or the schedules for the day.

Remember one of the rogue leadership principles we looked at earlier: what *happens* at meetings, interactions, or conversations—how you show up—matters much more than the framework you set up. You need to be more than active—you must also pay attention to the quality of action.

Let's look at a typical structured part of our business— the daily meetings we choose to schedule. While the schedule provides structure, it may not be the best way to ensure you are hitting the right notes.

Guidelines for Every Meeting

1. Decide who should be there and who shouldn't.

2. Look for opportunities to "cross-pollinate" ideas and people to create more synergy.

3. Decide how best to conduct the meeting.

4. Rotate roles at meetings, rather than always having the same people doing the same thing.

5. Clarify how you share the accountability.

6. Identify KPIs and decide on your format.

7. Focus on solutions instead of on problems.

8. Orchestrate meetings to leverage the collective brain trust.

9. Remain flexible—be prepared to change the format to drive a different outcome.

10. Clarify the purpose for each meeting.

11. Step back and ask these core questions:

   - What will I get out of this action, meeting, or scheduled event?

   - How does this action serve me?

   - Why are we here?

   - What outcome do we want or expect?

   - What's important to us? How will we discuss important issues and in what form?

   - How does the action serve my team? Can we do it differently to change the outcome?

   - What return on investment of time do my team and I get or expect?

- Can I get the same outcome by doing something else or using another method?

- Do I need to be present for this meeting or can I show up every now and then and still guide the group?

Repeat the messages you want to convey at each interaction—whether in a formal meeting or a chat in the hallway. Think of it like a long-term inoculation to ensure consistency.

Eventually, hand over the reins for the meeting to others. Your team should be able to run the meetings effectively without you when, for whatever reasons, you can't join them.

Stand-up meetings are great because they ensure less time sitting (and are therefore good for your health), but they don't guarantee important encouragement and support.

Here's how one of my clients, a major airline in Florida uncovered the key to effective use of meeting time.

The company had instituted a business review meeting, whereby managers and supervisors would get together on all three shifts to look at performance, plan the month ahead, solve problems together, and take actions.

The meetings created a wonderful forum for aligning the teams, developing a common messaging from leadership, and working on tasks together, not separately.

Too often, the shift teams did their own thing without connecting to the other shifts, and as a result, they often unintentionally affected overall team performance.

At the airline, weekly business review meetings became very successful, but then they began to take on a life of their own. Over time, they became two-hour sessions that didn't accomplish much.

New leaders swooped in and got rid of these ineffective meetings entirely. They failed to determine the original purpose for the meetings or if the workforce got any value out of them. As it turned out, the mid-level managers and supervisors missed having face time with their leaders to discuss business together.

The new leadership listened to the feedback and formulated a new agenda for the meetings, limiting them to only an hour, with a strict focus on performance reviews and recognition of accomplishments and right actions. The new business review meetings succeeded in driving performance improvements and team integration.

Rogue leaders envision impact. They cultivate awareness beyond the usual day-to-day perspective and make sure they add value and not just take action for its own sake.

One of the best strategic thinkers I have worked with was previously mentioned: John Kurz. He could see the connection between his daily responsibilities and the future of his company, constantly asking himself, "Do my actions work for the benefit of the organization?" Always acting with purpose, he actively sought feedback and patiently moved his organization forward.

THE GOLD MINE IN YOUR BACKYARD

Frontline and Middle Managers

It is better to lead from behind and to put others in front, especially when you celebrate victory when nice things occur. You take the front line when there is danger. Then people will appreciate your leadership.

—Nelson Mandela, world leader

To measure the quality of your leadership. you only need one yardstick. *What did you and your team accomplish?* Of course, no leader "is an island"—no leader operates alone. All his or her achievements involve dedicated teamwork. Leaders succeed by giving their people the space to succeed—to excel, grow, create, innovate, and overcome obstacles. That's your main purpose. So, let's tackle the platitudes right now . . .

1. Results measure success. Perhaps . . . but what did you leave on the table? What potential went unrealized? Did you create intrinsic value—*quality* and not just quantity?

2. Leaders are born, not made. Yep and yep. Leaders who surround themselves with people with great minds who challenge the status quo will grow and do better.

3. Leadership requires respect. True, but it also needs influential feedback and input. Great leaders make sure they have robust relationships with influencers at all levels of the organization—they help move your agenda forward.

4. Leading by example means highly visible action. Make sure to avoid atypical or grandiose gestures. Smaller examples introduced into daily conversations make leadership by example more effective long term.

5. Leaders must be decisive. Not true all the time. An effective leader sets up an inclusive decision-making process that strengthens the outcome.

6. Leaders need to have authority. Not true. As noted above, they need respect and influence. Look at Richard Nixon's cabinet in the final days. His team had set up a parallel system to work around him because they had lost faith in his credibility and decision-making. JFK did the same, setting up an alternative system to sideline his CIA chief during the Bay of Pigs crisis.

7. Leadership is about success. Leadership is also about how you act in complex and difficult times—for example, not just seizing a market opportunity, but also avoiding a disaster for the business.

8. Aim for the bottom line always. Most heroes remain hidden in untold stories. Being invisible and helping your organization, team, or group thrive takes some real power and focus. Coach Bobby Hurley of Saint Anthony's High School basketball team, a great example of an effective leader, talked more about college degrees, careers, and good citizenship—not wins. Yes, he won a lot of championships, but his greatness shines through from his wider focus. Think about the leaders in your life who continue to influence you to this day without even being present. To me, that reveals a greater measure of success.

9. Servant leadership as a badge. You serve shareholders. You serve clients. You serve your employees. If you want to lead, you have to understand it is not about *you*—although, of course, you have a lot to do with the outcome. Let the results speak for themselves.

10. Reward team loyalty. This cliché qualifies as a bunch of BS in so many ways. This phrase often gets used to extract more work from employees, but I have rarely seen it pay off for them. "War is old men talking and young men dying," as Brad Pitt declared in the film *Troy*. Nevertheless, if everyone—from the top down—pulls their weight and supports one another, then magic can happen.

Leaders need people to lead. And this takes us to the final piece of the puzzle: the forgotten middle managers and front liners—the people you really serve.

In reality, you don't lead—and you don't achieve anything—without the people you lead. Simple and basic, but often forgotten when the ego of "I'm in charge" dominates. Don't get fooled by the illusion.

Rogue leaders know that results are not their own but shared. As a leader, you have a single role to play. You can be effective or not. You can be inspirational or not. You can be focused or not. It's up to you.

36

SPARKING YOUR TEAM

Flipping the Pyramid

Today no leader can afford to be indifferent to the challenge of engaging employees in the work of creating the future. Engagement may have been optional in the past, but it's pretty much the whole game today.

—Gary Hamel, author

The crusty welding supervisor looked me up and down, and as he turned away, he let one fly, the spittle landing at my feet. "No f**ing way are you going to coach me." And he walked away.

Off to a flying start the first week as a coach at the shipyard. While his fellow supervisor and I stared at him incredulously, I fought my primal reaction, which was to scream loudly and say something very *Scarface*-like: "You talking to me?" I turned to John, smiled, and said, "I have him right where I want him." I knew I didn't sound convincing, but I had to control my impulses and not back down.

The odds of my actually forming a trusting coaching relationship with Mark, a hard-nosed thirty-year veteran who had a year until retirement, were steep.

My instincts told me he was afraid I would mess up his last year of his working life with "soft people focused on namby-pamby-mumbo jumbo," as he put it. I had some digging to do.

I discovered some interesting facts about him. His team loved him for his experience. He spent time with them on the boat while they worked their craft, instead of in his office. He dropped F bombs all the time. He was a lone wolf. He had survived by being a hard ass. Technically, he was a great welder, but a lousy communicator about performance.

Instead of asking permission, I showed up to his morning team meeting.

"Who invited you?" he grumpily demanded when I strolled into his work area.

"Your team told me you ran a great meeting, and I came to see how you do it." Resigned, he let me stay—to one side as an observer. I saw a natural leader who needed some help to talk about performance in a clear way.

Afterwards, I congratulated him on a wonderful meeting. I asked him about his team and what he thought they excelled at and could improve on. "Can I help you make it even better?" Knowing that he struggled with numbers, I offered to set up a self-calculating graph for him in Excel. All he needed to do was plug in the numbers.

He reluctantly agreed and came to appreciate the help. For the next year, I would swing by his meetings, and he would ask for feedback on how he was doing.

I worked with Mark for a year. He used his graphs diligently and became a better leader for it. When he retired, he didn't mention me in his "thank-yous." And he never apologized.

Was the partnership successful? Absolutely. We found a common, if not small, space that worked for both if us. He had changed and grown, even though he would never admit it. Most important, we respected each other. I am as proud of that achievement as one of the bigger, more visible wins for the shipyard. And that's nothing to spit at.

I learned a valuable lesson from this, something I want to share with all managers: Find a way to engage your front line in a meaningful way—not the "let's do a flip chart and thank you for your input" approach. Unfortunately, many leaders throw around words such as "engagement" and "empowerment," yet their actions hardly go beyond inviting employees to a meeting every now and then. To work at all, "empowerment" really needs to mean giving up control and decision-making power to others.

One truth remains constant in any business: Given the chance, the frontline team will grasp things quicker than the leadership. The higher up you go the corporate ladder, the more baggage and fear you encounter, resulting in rigid behaviors.

TEAR UP THOSE ANNUAL REVIEWS

Look for ways to foster feedback and dialogue with your frontline team, creating opportunities that allow you to give feedback too.

One way most organizations check the box is through the annual review process, which can help you shape your team and coach them. But make sure you also initiate an immediate response loop between you and your employees. Most information needs to be delivered and addressed well before the once-a-year ritual, when it's too late for the employee to make any adjustments. You are throwing away the opportunity to realize potential.

The longer the time between action and feedback, the less effective the feedback is for driving performance. Think about training a dog: If you wait two months (two hours!) to correct him after he behaves a certain way, he'll never change his behavior.

Improvement requires continuous feedback—not some flip chart exercise (with food catered by that really crappy sandwich place down the road). Try this with your team members:

1. Thank them for that great idea in the moment.

2. Ask them to speak to the team.

3. Pull them aside afterwards and tell them what went well and what can be improved.

4. As you end every meeting, review what you liked and what you would like to see done differently in the future.

5. Ask for feedback in public to model that it's okay.

6. Drop by for five minutes to talk to someone you don't know well on the team.

7. Eat lunch with the workforce—not some "special lunch with management" program. Just stroll in and share that bologna on white bread with someone.

8. Stay in touch with your influencers and keep them in the loop.

9. Be firm in private. Public floggings belong with the Marquis de Sade.

10. Show that feedback is safe and not personal.

THE POWER OF BEER

A customer waited on a delivery of doors to open a new facility on the weekend. The installation team had been unable to locate them, so the sales director asked the warehouse supervisor to solve the problem and take care of the customer. He even promised some beer if the supervisor could fix the problem.

The warehouse supervisor called the director later that night to say they had tracked down the doors—they had been on the wrong truck, going in the wrong direction.

Taking a risk, wanting to make sure the doors arrived in time, the supervisor signed off on a special delivery—beyond his level of authorization. Later that Friday evening, the director turned up at the warehouse, in the rain, with a case of beer for a very surprised supervisor.

Here was action that not only supported the front line, but also sent a strong message to the workforce about serving the customer and recognizing heroic work.

LEADERSHIP ASSASSINS

Types of Leaders Who Can Kill the Front Line

I am not afraid of an army of lions led by a sheep;
I am afraid of an army of sheep led by a lion.

—Alexander the Great, ancient Greek king

Before we wrap up, here is a list of the top enemies to successfully engaging the front line. Do a self-check, and ensure you are not unintentionally getting in your own way.

1. Big Daddy/Big Momma

Leaders whine and moan about having to make all the decisions—*precisely because they make all the decisions.* If employees know their bosses will take care of everything for them, then the result is usually passivity about decision-making, enabling the leader to continue his or her big-daddy behavior.

Leaders at all levels need to be freed to leverage their energy and actions. By taking care of others at a level below their pay grade, they end up impeding productivity and progress.

2. Chameleon

These leaders always take on the latest initiative—usually with fanfare (see chapter 18, "Stealth Change Management"). We have all experienced flavor-of-the-month initiatives and how organizations complain about all the energy expended for very little return. Instead of always going for the next-new-thing, managers typically do much better by adopting a slow-and-steady approach.

3. The King

Easy one to spot: "I am the leader, so I must be right." "Execute my vision" turns the workforce and your team into worker bees and drones, not "honey makers."

4. Policy Wonk

Nothing ever remains solid and static—as molecules vibrate, so do organizations. If you overdo policies and procedures, you risk squashing opportunities for growth and innovation.

5. The Fearmonger

These leaders dwell on crises, spending hours evaluating, delaying, pondering, and thinking about getting input—until the next big disaster comes to town. Afraid of making a mistake, they almost never do—which is itself a mistake. And the message to the front line? Usually paralysis.

6. The Hierarchist

Everyone has a boss. Though managing upward and externally does take time and skill, it hurts the front line when they focus more on what those above think than on what those in the trenches think.

If you truly want to "flip the pyramid" of management, then do so—but spend most of your time with those who can give you the best value and insight. To look only upward and outward harms business in the long term.

7. The Fixer

The general manager of a fish food plant visited the shop floor every week, but only to point out failures and to remind his workers who was boss. He focused on "fixing his people," not on fixing his style or his senior team's impact on the bottom line. Managing by walking around, in and of itself, does not improve management.

As noted previously, managers need to not only "show up," but also pay attention to *how* they show up to the front line. Meaningful conversations lead to improvement ideas from the workforce.

8. The Illusionist

The need to really connect to the workforce shows up most clearly in continuous improvement programs. Many CI programs fail because management invites the front line for their ideas but offers no follow up or feedback. As a result, many workers contribute only mediocre ideas or stop sharing input altogether.

9. One-Trick Pony

Because of the Deepwater Horizon catastrophe in 2010, oil company safety protocols shifted dramatically, and companies became focused on risk-control despite its impact on profitability. While the companies became safer, they also became somewhat risk averse.

That blindness meant they lost money elsewhere in the form of hidden costs. "We will get there by being safe" replaced "We will get there by being safe and profitable." On any journey, you have to make space for creativity, for adjustments—for "deviations from the path" if conditions demand it.

I call this "flex-rigidity"; others call it "agility." The outcome may even change—another good reason why mission and vision statements belong on walls and not in everyday work. Business environments remain too fluid for written-in-stone missions.

RECAP
Part 8: Engaging the Front Line

1. Plan with all your stakeholders (not just with employees)—a great resource for insight.

2. Be the conductor in charge of the business rhythm. If you aren't hitting the right notes, switch the tempo.

3. Help your front line understand the business case and let them take a bigger role in managing and executing.

4. Stay aware that most frontline teams will adapt to change faster than senior executives.

5. Follow up with the team on any ideas they have contributed.

6. Know who your influencers are at each level and area.

7. Be authentic and hold people accountable without punishment.

EPILOGUE
A Personal Note

We have reached the end of the rogue leadership journey. I hope you found it helpful and gleaned some ideas to help you on your way.

We will succeed or fail by how well we help our people achieve both personal and organizational goals. Results really do matter. We need to evaluate our actions based on outcomes and impact.

The *quality* of our actions can make a decisive difference. This requires us to act with integrity and authenticity so we can to tap into our natural and instinctive power.

To optimize this instinctive power, as a rogue leader you need to remove yourself from the fast-paced, demanding, and noisy world. Doing so, you open up a clearer channel for decision-making and creativity, enhancing how you respond to business challenges.

Rogue leadership is about stepping back and not engaging, allowing us to eventually engage more effectively. We have seen the power of reflection, of solitude, and of instinct—most of which are counterintuitive in the face of a never-ending assault of information and external stimuli demanding our immediate attention and response.

Understanding that we have more control over the environment than we typically acknowledge—plus the fact that we can change our brain states—helps us adapt to changing circumstances. We don't have to be victims of what happens; instead, we can tap into our innate power and ability to take charge of what needs to be accomplished. Too often, though, we default to the tail wagging the dog.

The outside environment triggers us before we've had the chance to really think about what the right response might be. While sometimes we have to make a decisive call on the spot, most of the time that's not even necessary or urgent.

False detours can distract us at any stage in the journey. Processes, tools, initiatives, and philosophies (such as Six Sigma and continuous improvement) can help—but only if you fully leverage their potential. No tool or technology works as a panacea. Go against the grain by questioning the value of all that you and your team do.

Once you are ready to engage in the outer world, focus on *purpose* as a key theme. Whether triage and decision-making, communicating, motivating your organization or team, or creating a powerful presence (both when physically on site and when away), make sure to hold a clear purpose in mind. Don't just act but *act consciously with purpose and intention* to achieve your goals, and consistently.

Continually take the pulse of your organization, get feedback, create opportunities for play to increase innovation, take calculated risks, and challenge the status quo. Think of yourself as a rebel leader *with* a cause.

Finally, understand that the key to your success is not you. Your workforce or team adds value (or unintentionally reduces value) every day—and when they are truly plugged in, your company's performance will improve.

The head winds will take you far. Build a unique shared story together, and, above all, have some fun doing so.

THE PATH TO SUCCESS

What Global Leaders Think

I asked my colleagues and clients from around the world to tell me what they see as the top characteristics of a transformative, effective leader. Their personalized feedback is a treasure of wisdom and experience, which I am humbled by.

> Throughout my experience, I have found that one of the most important things for any leader is to learn something new every day. You have to shape who you are, based on your circumstances, no structure or individual can be defined by the set of predefined regulations. I always give a high rate of independence to my team, which enables the individuals to grow at their own pace, gain confidence and stick together as a team. Success of the team is what makes an effective leader, person who leads his team toward a successful definition of themselves.
>
> **—Mamuka Bakhtadze, Prime Minister, Georgia**

The difference between leadership and management is a leader charts the course and a manager steers the ship. Developing leadership capability is a lifelong journey of discovery because there is always something more to learn— new skills, new techniques, new tools, new understanding. Leading people is so challenging yet so rewarding because of the inherent complexities built into leading people and into groups—the individuals and the interactions between individuals and within teams are all different and always changing and evolving, as is the external environment.

Becoming a great leader is analogous to becoming great in a new sport—you must practice small things every day and learn new skills and techniques to become a superior athlete; it's the same requirement to become a great leader.

—John Kurz, Fortune 500 Executive

The successful leader of the future drives the emerging regenerative economy through sustainable and human-centric innovative business practices. To do so successfully, leaders must have systemic thinking and sensing capabilities, complex global solution generation, and a moral compass ensuring responsible, aligned action for positive impact. A regenerative leader and business regenerates life. In short, such leaders give more than they take. To become a regenerative leader requires going against the grain of "business as usual," where profit maximization at the expense of environmental resources and human health and well-being is the norm. It requires a courageous commitment to use one's power consciously and develop lifelong practices of self-disruption of our habitual and unconscious mindsets and preconceived ideas and feeling impulses. This is leadership for the responsible, strong, and able-minded, and it requires deep inner work over a sustained period of time. It becomes a way of life that sustains and nourishes at the deepest level.

—Sandja Brügmann, Managing Partner,
the Passion Institute

The key to successful leadership is the ability to convey trust and honesty to the people who comprise your team, which in turn creates and breeds honor. Trust is one of the most valuable human assets and is earned over time—while honesty is the foundation in which great leadership can be attained. These two important components create the roots of the "culture of a company," which is essential for success. A business environment that operates with a rich culture establishes a veil of honor that is the oxygen of a successful company. Great leadership establishes this kind of playing field—honesty, trust, and honor—which gives everyone the ability to succeed on their own while strengthening any "weak links" that will appear. Great leadership can be measured by the success of a company because both go hand in hand.

—**Steele Platt, Founder, Yard House**

After twenty years working as an executive coach to Fortune 100 leaders there is one undeniable truth I have uncovered, "you can't win at life if you are losing in your mind" and therein lies the difference between authentic leaders and those who follow the masses. Leaders who inspire those around them must possess certain key characteristics to be successful, such as a high level of EQ, to fight the daily battles that face them, but more important is the battle within. Authentic leaders know when and how to call bulls*t on themselves by asking themselves powerful questions that challenge their internal beliefs. To lead in the twenty-first century (and beyond) leaders must come to understand who they are, what they stand for, and what they are capable of providing those they lead.

—**Joshua Miller, master certified executive coach, author,**
Amazon best seller *I Call Bullshit: Live Your Life,*
Not Someone Else's

Leadership is about taking initiative—pioneering progress, catapulting projects, and engaging people to do
their best work. If you are in a leadership role, you must
be an initiator who is capable of moving an organization
forward.

—**Jimmy Calano, Founder and CEO (retired),**
CareerTrack

My best advice is this: When delegating, prioritize assigning tasks according to strengths and weaknesses. The
company won't benefit from having a team member
completing a task they don't feel confident in. Delegate
wisely and play to people's strengths to obtain the best
results. This goes the same for yourself—if your skills
could be better put to use elsewhere, don't be afraid to
let go of the reins and focus on growth.

—**Candice Galek, Founder, Bikini Luxe**

Decision-makers aren't cold, calculating, dispassionate
machines; they're human beings. And human beings
are notoriously bad for making critical decisions based
on what they feel in their gut instead of what the data
reveals. They may know facts and figures but can choose
to ignore scientific findings if their feelings tell them
otherwise. Your job as a leader is to connect with the
workforce on a personal level. Get as deep as you can in
finding their trigger points so they will pay attention to
your message. Get them to see the true meaning of what
you can deliver, and not just superficial bullet points
that dance around the core of what you offer. At the very
least, create communications that speak directly to their
ambitions, aspirations, desires, and fears. Don't be afraid

to strike an emotional chord. Get them to care about what it is you have to tell them. Deliver meaning.

—**Frank Pietrucha, President, Definitive Communications, and author,** *Supercommunicator: Explaining the Complicated So Anyone Can Understand*

Emphasize the care that must be taken with the people, the work team, on the road to the achievements that the leader challenges the team to achieve. There is a high risk of falling into pressures bordering on excessive imposition or so-called motivation at the expense of employees' self-esteem. A good leader must above all be clear about what should move the business and the people and what should be avoided. Leading is to show the way, communicate and share the vision, let the team grow and mature, and bring out the best in each one to achieve it. It is essential to have a sense of humor to overcome difficult moments, unplanned adverse events, and bring creativity to solutions.

The fact that the team feels that "it can go with its leader into battle," feeling such a loyalty and admiration for the "Boss," is what generates the bonds to surpass what was believed possible and creates results better than expected.

—**Alejandra Sabugo, Gerente de Administracion, CMPC Tissue**

I believe you have to surround yourself with the smartest people you can find, never feel like you have to have all the answers, let your people know how important their work and contributions are to the organization, give them a vision of where you want the organization to head, then let them do their job to achieve that goal! Support and encouragement along the way are critically important. Leaders have to earn trust and respect—it's all about people and capturing their hearts, as well as their minds.

—Becky Stewart, Retired VP, Fortune 500

I didn't set out to become a leader, but rather to do whatever I could to make things better. I have always approached my role as being in a better position to help remove the obstacles that get in the way of the workforce. That's my role.

—Roy Fonseca, Terminal Manager, American Airlines, Miami International Airport

I think the key is to be able to see and grasp opportunities today without overwhelming yourself with long-term career paths. Take opportunity, do whatever you do with passion and dedication, and these will take care of longer-term success. And another one is "Do invest in people who work for you, as we are only as good as they are."

—Leyla Novruzova, VP HR, Fortune 500

I would offer that keeping your head up, keeping eyes on the market and strategy as well as inside the organization, and relentless execution are the keys. One day I will figure out how to do all that.

—Tim Taylor, President and CEO, FreeFlight Systems

If I had to give one piece of effective leadership advice it would be the insight that when it comes to motivating people to execute projects, it is better to inspire them to action, rather than having them implement action. People will always be more motivated to work on something that is "theirs." When you inspire people to action, their work productivity will increase because they are doing it from their fuel source, not ours. How do I execute that? My rule of thumb is to make sure everyone who works for my company is pursuing their dream under the umbrella of my company. When they pursue their dream and leave their mark of excellence, inspiration is a no brainer.

—**Tracy Kemble, PhD, Owner, Dr. Tracy TV and Mrs. Globe**

Organizations that can create truly sustainable performance will be the winners of tomorrow. This requires leaders and teams who can adapt and learn quickly, who can instigate and sustain change in a complex system in which they have significantly less direct control, who can establish a creative and innovative environment in which solutions are swiftly arrived at, and who can ensure a high order of person and collective well-being deep into their organizations in which the work is felt to be positive and have real meaning.

In short, it will require leaders to establish modern learning organizations, or as we say, organizations who know how to "slow down to speed up."

—**David Webster, Director, Centre for Teams, London**

The French poet Nicolas Boilleau said that we must listen to the earth. She is our only common home and she is weakened by our actions, but she has an incredible weapon—resilience. Every human being who listens to his heart knows how important it is to preserve our beautiful environment for our own survival.

—Cyrielle Hariel,speaker, journalist, and author, *Faire battre le cœur du monde*

Leadership is most effective when you have developed and shared a clear vision with all employees in your organization. Through this you can create a culture of empowerment and enhanced self-confidence which will result in the breakdown of barriers leading to an environment of honesty and openness. As a leader I always believed in the untapped potential of all employees and believed my role was to create an environment in which they could realize this potential. A good leader must be a good listener and be able to relate to every employee.

—Ken McKenzie, Retired Sr. VP, Premdor Europe

The most important quality for a leader is to speak passionately from the heart; to be authentic and to see all people as equal. Ultimately a great leader has reached a state of deep compassion for all fellow human beings.

—Lady Louisa Compton, humanitarian

Leaders create the culture and the culture creates results. Within every organization there lives a culture that either works for them or works against them—the difference between a success and nurturing culture and one of disappointment and dysfunction. As a first step, you need take the temperature of your organization on a regular basis to ensure that it is performing at an optimum level. This also allows you to take a read on how individual employees are performing . . . are they just showing up and going through the motions or are they fully engaged and excited to be there? If those two statements are the bookends of corporate culture then regularly tracking the temperature will be a significant performance indicator for you. Accountability should not be viewed as a punishment but rather as an indicator to track and measure performance.

—**John Rose, leadership succession/transition/ culture expert, John Rose Consulting**

The adoption of new technology change people's behavior which puts totally new demands on leaders and their teams. On how they interact with their customers, how they inform, how fast they are, but also on how products and services are designed. In the light of the fast-paced change we see today the leadership must adopt and change accordingly. The importance of a high Adaptability Quotient (AQ), rather than a high EQ or IQ, increases and can differentiate a corporation from another.

And are we managing for today or for tomorrow? A company's long-term survival often depends on taking risks, experimenting and learning from failure in the hunt for new products, services, and processes. At the same time, a company also needs consistency and attention to make the most out of the existing products, services, and processes they already have. These innovation paradoxes can bring tensions between today and tomorrow. An effective leader needs to take into account a "both/and" leadership to be successful.

—**Annelie Gullström, global digital transformation expert and strategist**

The future starts today, not tomorrow!

—Cormac McConnell, CEO,
Common Good International

Good leadership is not about power. It's about trust. I always try to inspire and motivate people to feel good about themselves, confident enough to take the necessary steps, willing and wanting to trust themselves and their instincts. It is important that people feel safe and that they can trust me, and they only do so if I trust them, listen to them, and leave enough space which includes them. Everyone needs to understand the context and be respected and acknowledged. I always try to listen, honor, and appreciate everyone and at the same time listen, honor, and appreciate myself.

—Eva Helmersson, inspirational innovator,
influencer, patient advocate

There is no recipe for leadership. There is a journey, where you can try, learn, get inspired, try again, get feedback, fail, do your best, learn, and try some more. Best anchors on the journey are personal values, principles, asking for feedback, and an open heart.

—Anja Voss, global executive trainer and facilitator

There will always be leaders and followers. It is the duty of the leader to create new leaders when possible and nurture followers toward success in their collaborate mission.

—John M. Freeborn, Director, iST Gateway LLC

Good leaders bring visions to life. They know that everything they need resides inside of them. Epic leaders know when to lead and when to follow. They are unique humans who follow their heart regardless of what society says they should do.

Phenomenal leaders see the good in all walks of life, so they experience great defeat that prepares them for their destiny. They do their best to learn from mistakes even if it takes a while. The best leaders live to make the world a better place by being the love they wish to see in the world.

—Tsailii J. Rogers, entrepreneur, producer,
actress, and philanthropist

Leaders are those who know that success is not a lucky moment. For them success is discipline plus consistency and hard work. The true leaders are those who motivates others and shows them the path they would walk together to succeed. When they achieve their goals, they don't use "I"—they say, "We."

—Inna Boyadzhieva, crowdfunding expert

My key to effective leadership: Leadership is not about being at the forefront of change, it's being the energy that drives that change. That energy can only be found by harnessing our integrity, creativity, emotional intelligence, and authenticity. Effective leadership comes from the congruency of channeling these essences of our human nature, emanating from your innermost self and letting them direct you.

—Caroline McMenamin, Founder,
Replenish: Acting on Mental Health

I was always encouraged to identify and develop folks with leadership potential and I did the same. Investment here is more important than plant and equipment. First line and middle management leaders are the ones who have the toughest challenges. They need the most support. But, unless you identify and deal with the actively disengaged in your organization—not necessarily poor performers, but the folks who deliberately undermine the leaders— it's tough for the organization to excel. Help them change or purge them.

—Irwin F. Edenzon, Retired President,
Ingalls Shipbuilding

The ultimate goal of true leadership is not to maintain control over people but to produce leaders and people greater than yourself.

—Tiffany Sonnier, International Executive Director,
Destiny Institute

Leadership:

- Win the hearts and minds of people
- Culture Culture Culture
- Transparency
- Approachable
- Good listener
- Questions
- Great GUT
- People person

—Jimmy L. Johns, Vice President, Site Lead,
Elbit Systems of America

I find that with a good work environment and a team that works well, we can achieve excellent business results. Qualities such as competence, values, a positive attitude, and consequential behavior are the basics.

—**Sergio Alvarez, Gerente General,**
Forestal Bosques del Plata

Leadership starts with authenticity and the ability to relate. Win your people's respect and their desire to "want to," and the other necessary leadership traits then impact your company's desired results exponentially and sustainably.

—**Joseph Starcevic, Principal,**
Joseph Starcevic Business Coach Inc.

Leadership inspires not only the mindset but the heartset as well. This way team members are courageous, they feel positivity, connected and supported to unleash their potential, creating value and achieving meaningful results.

—**Zita Gaál, Executive and Team Coach,**
M&G Vision Coaching

It's obvious that leadership requires confidence, but all too often in contemporary business culture, we mistake the traits of arrogance, inflexibility, and self-congratulations for confidence. I prefer to see the confidence of a leader reflected as commitment to the mission of the organization and to the people entrusted to carry it out. Leaders who exhibit this commitment are not devoid of ego, but rather gain their reward from the accomplishments of the organization as a whole, and from the team of people who make it happen, as opposed to the praise (and sometimes fear) that is directed at themselves.

—**Tony Shaw, CEO and Founder, Dataversity**

ABOUT THE AUTHOR

Paul Rosenberg is an award-winning, transformational leadership coach, senior executive, and performance consultant with over thirty years of experience. Having worked and lived on every continent except Antarctica, he offers a unique global skill set that cuts across boundaries and industries.

His diverse clients have included global leaders and Fortune 500 companies like American Airlines, Honeywell, and Premdor/Masonite, as well as NGOs, start-ups, and greenfield/first-to-market entrepreneurs.

Previously, Paul led marketing and business development in Chile, Sweden, New Zealand, Spain, Mexico, and the former USSR.

As a stand-up comic and former improvisational actor, he brings an innovative approach to business. Paul is a sought-after speaker, trainer, and facilitator in creativity, culture, and performance.

He holds a BA in Mass Communications/Sociology (University of Denver) and an MBA (California Lutheran University). He also has grad school credits at the University of Wisconsin in case anyone is counting. He is bilingual in Spanish and English.

Paul lives in South Florida with his wife, Mauge, where it's way too hot in August.

⌂ www.rosenbergpaul.com
in https://www.linkedin.com/in/paul-rosenberg-69a2a9/
▣ https://www.instagram.com/paulrosenberg_/
▢ @PaulRosenberg_
f https://www.facebook.com/RogueLeadership/

Made in the USA
Middletown, DE
04 December 2018